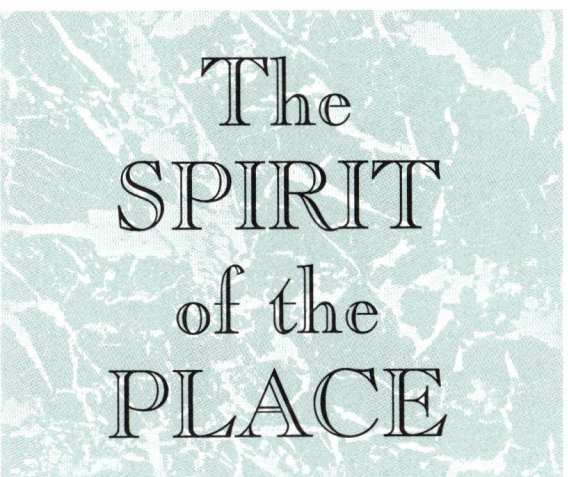

The SPIRIT of the PLACE

Florida's

EMERALD COAST

*Celebrates Its Finest Restaurants,
Chefs, and Cuisine*

Written and Compiled by Kurt R. Niland & J. Scott Armstrong
Illustrated by Bruce Ward

ISBN 0-9645334-0-5

Library of Congress Catalog Card Number pending

Oracle Publishing Company, L.C.
P.O. Box 1741
Santa Rosa Beach, Florida 32459

Printed in Canada
First Edition

Front Cover: Looking toward East Pass from Destin Bridge
Back Cover: White sand and sea oats
Photographs by David Shea Studios, Ft. Walton Beach, FL.
Book Design: Katherine M. Harris

The Artist...

The sketches in this book were drawn by Bruce Ward. Born in Mobile, Alabama and now residing in Montgomery, Mr. Ward is owner of Visual Images, a design studio in Montgomery that specializes in custom automotive and nautical lettering and art, sign making, and logo design and illustration. We are fortunate to have Mr. Ward's work in *The Spirit of the Place: Emerald Coast*. So rarely have we found an artist who can so successfully translate what is in the mind's eye to ink and paper, or any other medium. Thanks Bruce!

Thanks...

We at Oracle Publishing would like to thank our family, friends, and associates whose enthusiasm and support have been crucial to the creation of this book: Melissa Armstrong (for dedication, Santa visits, and a view of the moon over Georgia); Emily Armstrong (also known as "Tweety Bird"); Ray and Evelyn Niland (for the love and light they cast on life); Myers and Freida Armstrong (for genetically good sense); Todd, Tiffany, and Tanner Armstrong (whose time has come to realize who really is numero uno); Amy Page (the squid dancer extraordinaire); Forrest Page (a skinny kid with a big heart); Paul Stamler (responsible for Connecticut's gin shortages); Dr. Robert Evans and wife Ruth (friends, teachers, and mentors both); Neal and Sallie Spaulding ("As in music, so in life."); Liz Cameron (somewhere in England); Julianna Ooi (a good friend armed with seaweed, gun, *and* a thesis); Philip Ding (waterskis and all), William Shakespeare, John Keats, Alan Watts, God, and all the others who we see less often but whose wisdom, love, and friendship cannot go unrecognized. Thanks for your faith in us.

And More Thanks...

Our thanks also go out to all the great people in the business realm whose help and cooperation we deeply appreciate: the folks at SouthTrust Bank of Covington County; Donna Bailey (Sweet Basil's); Lilly Bass (Staff's); Jack Buchanan (La Pergola); Tim Creehan (Marina Cafe); Johnny Earles (Criolla's); Sheilah Hayward (Hatteras Cafe); Gary Serafin (Jamie's); Chester Kroeger (Fudpucker's); Suzy Lyons (McGuire's); Annie Mangrum (Flamingo Cafe); Bill Martin (Flounder's); the Patronis family (Captain Anderson's); Eloise Poole (Billy's); Billy Redd (Saltwater Grill); Bill Reider (Elephant Walk and Sunset Bay Cafe); Pat Scotto (Scotto's); Clark Williams (Captain Dave's); Gabby Woodward (Harbor Docks), and to all the chefs of these great restaurants whose culinary creations have inspired us to undertake this project.

Introduction

Take a culinary tour of the Emerald Coast's finest restaurants! All of the participating restaurants in the cookbook have submitted favorite recipes that collectively reflect what we call "The Spirit Of The Place." In determining which restaurants to include in this book, Oracle Publishing conducted extensive surveys of both locals and vacationers in the coastal counties from Pensacola to Panama City. This approach provided us with objective standards and prevented us from being food and restaurant critics, which admittedly we have no authority to be. The responses to our survey furnished us with a surprisingly eclectic list of restaurants that reflect a wide variety of incomes, tastes, geographical regions, and other criteria. We contacted the restaurants that were most frequently cited in the survey and asked them to submit recipes that best reflected their style and type of cuisine. Thus, whether one prefers home cooking or gourmet, French or Italian, Cajun or Caribbean, this cookbook is sure to contain recipes for every taste and budget. (Admittedly, we took a few liberties in defining which areas to cover in the Emerald Coast. Although the term traditionally encompasses the Destin and Ft. Walton Beach regions, the special qualities from which the "Emerald Coast" derives its name extend in both directions — specifically to Pensacola and Panama City. Moreover, there are some excellent, "must-visit" restaurants in those cities which are very much worth the drive for anyone vacationing in the Emerald Coast proper.)

Given the outstanding reputations of the participating restaurants, this cookbook could have easily assumed the title "People's Choice," "Award Winning Restaurants of the Emerald Coast," or "The Best of the Best." However, we sought a more encompassing title — one that would more completely describe the body of recipes and restaurant profiles in this book. After we collected and combined all of the information, we discovered that we had inadvertently tapped into what seemed to be the true spirit of the Emerald Coast. The Emerald Coast restaurants, with their myriad of cuisines, themes, architectural styles, and geographical settings, formed a microcosmic yet complete representation of the Emerald Coast itself. In effect, when you browse through *The Spirit Of The Place: Emerald Coast* and sample some of the recipes, we hope that you will recapture and re-experience the joy of life on the Emerald Coast (if you live elsewhere) or reacquaint yourself with the place that you know so well and love (if you are a local).

While many of the recipes in this cookbook come directly from the menu, many of them are time-tested family favorites submitted to us by the owners, proprietors, and chefs of the participating restaurants. In soliciting the recipes, our only criterion was that the restaurants send us their best; we did not request recipes of a particular category or ingredient. Thus, as you prepare the recipes in this book, you recreate dishes originally concocted by the Emerald Coast's (and the world's) most outstanding and imaginative chefs. We also wanted to meet the current demand for shorter, more concise specialty cookbooks filled with unique recipes, rather than publish a large collection of standard recipes. Because of its unique quality, you will find that the organization of *The Spirit of the Place: Emerald Coast* is different from other cookbooks. Instead of grouping all of the recipes by category (i.e., appetizer, entree, dessert, etc.), we divided the cookbook into restaurant sections and grouped each restaurant's recipes under its particular section. We then included a table of contents and two indexes (one by title and one by ingredient) to facilitate reference and diminish any problems that the organization of the book would otherwise incur.

Because most of the recipes in this cookbook were professionally developed and reduced from their original proportions, we encourage you to keep the following advice in mind when cooking: In doubling or in other ways increasing the serving size of a recipe, calculate the ingredients as necessary except for the seasonings. Increase all spices by a small fraction of what the original recipe requires and then gradually season to taste. Automatically doubling or tripling the amount of spices called for can distort or overpower the flavor of the dish.

When preparing these recipes, try to awaken the intuitive chef in you. Don't be afraid to experiment. If you do not like a particular ingredient, substitute something else for it and customize the recipes to your personal taste. Even if you dislike seafood, you can still use all of the recipes in this book by creatively replacing seafood ingredients with those that you do enjoy. Many great dishes were born through experimentation and substitution.

Several of the recipes and sub-recipes in this cookbook can be combined with other recipes. For example, a sauce that goes well with a particular dish may also complement another, or you may find that a particular cheesecake filling works better with the crust from a different recipe. To help you in your experimentation, we have broken down composite recipes by isolating their constituent parts, which we then labeled with a smaller typeface. Each crust, sauce, filling, and side dish is indexed as if it were a recipe in itself. Don't be afraid to use such recipes creatively whenever you cook.

Since most of the recipes in this book were developed by professional chefs, you may encounter some unfamiliar ingredients and preparation terms. We have made an effort to forestall any confusion by assembling a brief overview of terms and ingredients, which you can find in the "hints and tips" sections throughout the book. We encourage you to browse through these informative tips; all of them are immediately relevant to the preparation of the recipes in this book and they also offer a lot of valuable advice that can instantly increase your knowledge of cooking everything from the most common items to more exotic specialties.

One last word about ingredients: The majority of the recipes in this cookbook require ingredients that are easily recognizable and easily found. However, now and again a recipe may call for something which is not readily available. Should this happen, don't worry. If you live in a big city, chances are you can find anything you need at a gourmet shop or specialty market. If you live neither in a big city nor in the Emerald Coast and you want to make a recipe that calls for something not available locally, try the substitution method. Who knows, you may even wind up creating something unique and extra-ordinarily delicious!

Whatever and however you cook, we hope that you enjoy *The Spirit Of The Place: Emerald Coast*. Please watch for our second volume, which we are currently compiling in response to the demand for this type of cookbook. Volume II of *The Spirit Of The Place: Emerald Coast* will feature recipes from several other of the Emerald Coast's finest restaurants that were not able to participate in this edition. If you would like to see any other Emerald Coast restaurant or restaurants in the future volume, please let us know. We will be happy to follow your leads!

Table of Contents

Restaurant Addresses

Billy's I
Thomas Drive
Panama City Beach

Billy's II
East Highway 98
Seagrove Beach

Captain Anderson's
North Lagoon Drive & Thomas
Panama City Beach

Captain Dave's
East Highway 98
Destin

Criolla's
Highway 30A
Grayton Beach

Elephant Walk
East Highway 98
Sandestin

Flamingo Cafe
East Highway 98
Destin

Flounder's
Quiet Water Beach Road
Pensacola Beach

Fudpucker's
Highway 98
Destin

Fudpucker's
Santa Rosa Blvd.
Ft. Walton Beach

Harbor Docks
East Highway 98
Destin

Hatteras Cafe
East Highway 98
Destin

Jamie's
East Zaragoza Street
Pensacola

Marina Cafe
East Highway 98
Destin

McGuire's
East Gregory Street
Pensacola

La Pergola
Highway 30A
Blue Mountain Beach

Saltwater Grill
West Highway 98
Panama City

Scotto's
Alcaniz Street
Pensacola

Staff's
Miracle Strip Pkwy.
Ft. Walton Beach

Sunset Bay Cafe
East Highway 98
Sandestin

Sweet Basil's
East Highway 98
Destin

Sweet Basil's
West Highway 98
Panama City Beach

The Spirit of the Place: *Emerald Coast*

is dedicated with much love and thanks to the
Armstrong and Niland families.

*"I believe that more unhappiness comes from this source than
from any other - I mean from the attempt to prolong family
connection unduly and to make people hang together artifi-
cially who would never naturally do so."*

--Samuel Butler (1835-1902)

Foreword

The Emerald Coast is one of the most spectacular places on earth. Time and again I meet people who have left behind their own corners of the world to settle here, and I wonder how many vacationers head back home each year with the same intentions in mind. The reasons, perhaps, are simple. Once you witness the beauty of the Emerald Coast and experience what we call "the spirit of the place," you will indeed find it difficult to extricate yourself from its arresting charm.

First of all, there is the sand. Soft, dazzling, and brilliant white, it is a true miracle of nature. Surrealistically mistaken for snow by many a newly arrived visitor, especially in the half-light of a full moon, the sand is alone enough reason for thousands of people to visit the Emerald Coast. Then there is the ocean itself, which is more dynamic here than in most other regions of the globe. In its more turbulent days, the Gulf of Mexico dramatically churns with Emerald waves reminiscent of the open Atlantic. More often, however, the words 'Emerald Coast' seem a misnomer; the water turns a clear aqua color in calmer conditions, making the beaches as captivating as the palm-fringed lagoons of the Caribbean or South Pacific. Whatever its condition, the Gulf is always a colossal presence that roars in the background and influences every facet of life on the Emerald Coast.

But the beauty of the Emerald Coast extends beyond the immediate shoreline. Further inland, the terrain is alive with tangles of mossy oaks, ancient magnolias, wild palms, various pines, and banana trees. Lakes, bayous, and cool springs diversify the local landscape and its ecosystems. The presence of these natural elements is always near — hardly subdued and never eliminated by the bulldozer and crane, making it one of the last places where you can experience Florida in its uncorrupted and natural state.

The cities and villages of the Emerald Coast are also marked by tremendous social and cultural diversity. Some areas share an affinity with the Deep South and its traditions while others contain the bustling highways and glitzy strips more akin to South Florida. In a single day, one can also experience the remains of sixteenth century Spain in Pensacola, the Caribbean charm of Seaside, and the dizzying festivity of Cajun and Creole culture that has spilled into all parts of the Emerald Coast from South Louisiana.

Of course, any written description of a place must ultimately fall short of its aim to accurately grasp in words what perhaps only the physical senses may truly and fully experience. And perhaps it is for this reason that you can feel the "spirit of the place" even when you are not in the Emerald Coast by creating some of the dishes in this cookbook — dishes that some of the world's most outstanding chefs and restaurants have developed. We hope that you enjoy this book. And we hope that the spirit of the Emerald Coast fills your kitchen.

Kurt R. Niland
Destin, Florida

Grouper Salad Sandwich   Oyster Stew   French Bean and Corn Casserole
Hot Cheese and Crab Dip   Spirit Pie   Coconut Punch (Puerto Rican Egg Nog)

Billy's Steamed Seafood Restaurant, Oyster Bar, and Crab House

Panama City Beach, Florida / Seagrove Beach, Florida

One visit to Billy's Steamed Seafood Restaurant, Oyster Bar, and Crab House, and you'll understand why this Panama City Beach restaurant is so critically "esteamed." Called "congenial and solicitous" by the *New York Times*, praised in the pages of *Southern Living*, *Arthur Frommer's Florida Guidebook*, and *Travelhost* magazine, Billy's is a Florida treasure with a reputation that soars beyond the Emerald Coast.

Billy's is run by the Poole family, with Billy himself in the kitchen steaming up the best Florida blue crabs in town. His wife Eloise greets the guests while their lovely daughter Beth serves up the legendary food. This friendly family restaurant provides an atmosphere that is thoroughly genuine in all respects; it is a restaurant that truly captures the local spirit with a very casual atmosphere that echoes with the crackling of crab claws.

The recipes in this section were prepared by Eloise. You can find some of them on Billy's menu, while others are time-tested family favorites. The Oyster Stew and the Grouper Salad Sandwich are recipes that bid you to cook without measure, but we promise they are well worth the extra effort! (And besides, they're a lot of fun to prepare this way, and you may even develop a variation that is uniquely your own.) So put on your apron and start cooking. And, when you're in the Panama City Beach area, stop by either of Billy's locations and experience firsthand why the restaurant is so highly rated both by scores of customers and by national publications.

Grouper Salad Sandwich

"This salad can also be stuffed in a large fresh tomato and served on lettuce leaves, topped with a lemon slice, and served with chips on the side. If you make a sandwich, Eloise suggests topping it with sliced black olives."

1/2 pound fresh grouper, cooked	**Bell pepper, chopped**
Relish	**Onion, chopped**
Mayonnaise	**Salt and pepper**
Prepared mustard	**Onion salt**
Celery, chopped	**Juice of 1 fresh lemon**

Crumble fish and mix with relish and mayonnaise to desired consistency. Add approximately 1 tablespoon mustard, celery, bell pepper, onion, salt, pepper, onion salt, and the juice of a fresh lemon. Serve on toasted French bread topped with chopped scallions and paprika.

Yield is variable

Oyster Stew

12 oysters per bowl of stew	**Black Pepper**
Scallions, chopped	**Salt**
Celery, chopped	**Butter**
Parsley, chopped	**Whole milk or cream**
Garlic salt	**Paprika**
White pepper	**Tabasco sauce (optional)**

Open oysters, but do not wash. Toss chopped green scallions, celery, and parsley over oysters. Add a dash of garlic salt, white pepper, black pepper, salt, and butter. Steam until oysters curl. Add whole milk or cream and return to steamer. Heat thoroughly but do not boil. Sprinkle with paprika and parsley. A drop of Tabasco is optional. Add one dozen oysters to each bowl of stew.

Yield is variable

French Bean and Corn Casserole

1 can white whole kernel corn,
    drained
1 can French style beans
1 can cream of celery soup
$1/2$ pound cheddar cheese, grated
$1/2$ cup water chestnuts
$1/2$ cup onions, chopped
$1/2$ cup celery, chopped
$1/2$ cup green pepper, chopped

$1/2$ cup sour cream

Topping

1 stick oleo (margarine)
$1/2$ cup grated cheese
$1/2$ cup Ritz crackers, crushed
$1/2$ cup slivered almonds

Combine all ingredients (except for the topping) together in 3-quart greased casserole dish. Melt oleo and mix with cracker crumbs and almonds. Put on top of casserole. Sprinkle with Parmesan cheese. Bake for 45 minutes at 350 degrees.

Makes 1 (3-quart) casserole

Hot Cheese and Crab Dip

*"An outstanding dip that will surely become your own family's favorite.
Serve it with crusty bread, melba toast, or wheat wafers."*

$1/2$ pound lump crab meat, cooked
1 (10-ounce) package shredded
    sharp cheddar cheese

1 (8-ounce) package shredded
    mild cheddar cheese
$1/4$ cup butter
$1/2$ cup sauterne

Mix crab meat, cheese, butter, and sauterne in a sauté pan. Cook over a low heat, stirring continuously until cheese melts and substance is heated thoroughly. Pour into chafing dish.

Makes 3 cups

Spirit Pie

"So easy to make, that even a poor cook can't fail in creating this delicious dessert."

2 eggs
1 cup sugar
$1/2$ cup melted butter
3 tablespoons bourbon
1 tablespoon vanilla

$1/4$ cup corn starch
1 cup pecans, chopped
1 cup chocolate chips
1 graham cracker pie shell
Whipped cream

Mix first eight ingredients in mixing bowl, stirring as you add. Pour into graham crust pie shell and bake 45 minutes in a 350 degree oven. Let cool and top with whipped cream before serving.

Makes 1 pie

Coconut Punch (Puerto Rican Eggnog)

"The Poole family discovered this recipe while spending Christmas in Puerto Rico a few years ago. It is the island's answer to egg nog."

5 egg yolks
2 cans evaporated milk
14 ounces condensed milk
2 cans cream of coconut

1 (750-ml) bottle white rum
1 teaspoon vanilla extract
Dash of salt
Dash of cinnamon

Mix egg yolks and milk in blender. Add remaining ingredients and blend thoroughly. Refrigerate until well chilled. Serve with pineapple slice and cherries.

Makes approximately 2 quarts

The Emerald Coast Region

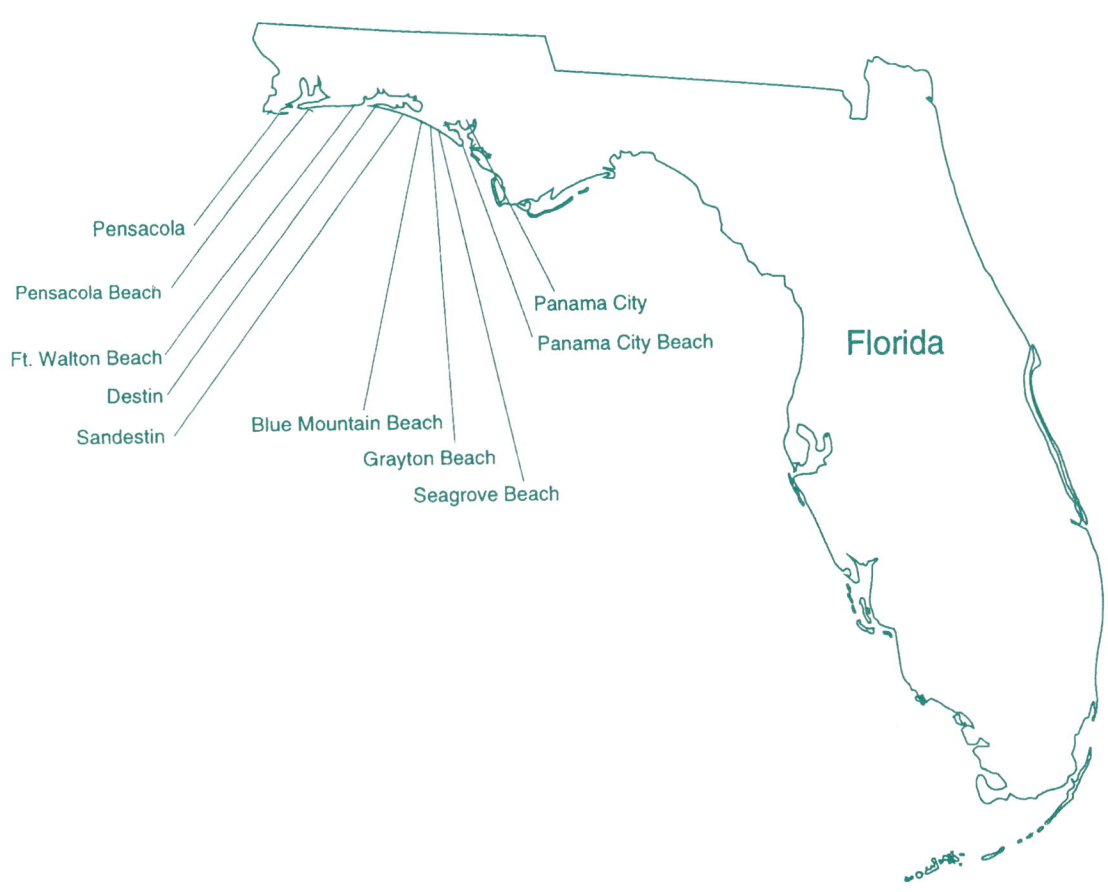

Pensacola

Pensacola Beach

Ft. Walton Beach

Destin

Sandestin

Blue Mountain Beach

Grayton Beach

Seagrove Beach

Panama City

Panama City Beach

Florida

Cuban Beans & Rice   Beer Battered Chicken   Shark Florida   Baked Fish
Be'chamel (White Sauce)   Grilled Shrimp   Tzatziki   Cole Slaw   Hush Puppies
Coconut Pie   Sweet Potato Pie   Coconut Candy

Captain Anderson's

Panama City Beach, Florida

Situated on Panama City Beach's Grand Lagoon, Captain Anderson's Restaurant is a big restaurant with an even bigger reputation. Currently ranked as one of the nation's top 50 restaurants and as one of Florida's top 10, Capt. Anderson's has received just about every award for restaurant excellence that exists, including the coveted Golden Spoon Award by *Florida Trend* magazine. The Patronis family attributes the tremendous success of their restaurant to "a passion for quality and a commitment to service," as well as a stern refusal to "operate [their] restaurant out of a freezer" despite the 300,000 dinners they serve in their nine months of operation each year. These high standards of culinary excellence and dedication to service have carried Capt. Anderson's through forty years of unrivaled success in the Florida Panhandle.

Behind the scenes, Capt. Anderson's displays admirable respect and conviction in protecting the natural environment, particularly the local waters where the Patronis family has witnessed a startling decrease in both the fish population and the variety of aquatic species that normally inhabits the coastal waters. Of course, the repercussions of overfishing could have a doleful impact on the restaurant industry, which Capt. Anderson's readily acknowledges. But more importantly, they acknowledge that "a dying ocean jeopardizes the very survival of this planet." This state of affairs has evoked what Capt. Anderson's calls a "Critical Imperative" to preserve the marine environment by employing saner, more responsible fishing practices and by refining development of the shoreline. It seems also to be their appeal to the human conscience over legal enactments, which have historically failed to bring about the much needed reversal of these destructive trends.

Perhaps the Patronis family's concern for the sea and their respect for its gifts are rooted in the seafaring traditions of Patmos, a Greek island of the Dodecanese archipelago. Back in 1913, Theo Patronis left his native Patmos to begin a new life in Tallahassee, Florida. There, he opened the Five and Ten (or "F and T") Restaurant near the state capitol, and for more than 50 years it stood as a popular hub for governors, legislators, businessmen, and civic leaders. Theo's sons Johnny and Jimmy followed his example when they opened the Seven Seas restaurant in downtown Panama City in 1953. Fourteen years later, they purchased Capt. Anderson's Restaurant which quickly blossomed into the legend that it is today.

Cuban Beans and Rice

"Traditionally named 'Moors and Christians,' this combination of beans and rice is a staple for Cubans. A squeeze of fresh lemon juice will do wonders to the flavor. Or, try serving it with a dash of mango chutney just before serving."

1 pound black beans	1 teaspoon chili powder
1$^{1}/_{2}$ quarts cold water	$^{1}/_{4}$ teaspoon cayenne
4 slices bacon, fried crisp	$^{1}/_{4}$ teaspoon salt
1 clove garlic, minced	1 quart meat stock
1 onion, diced	2 cups long-grain rice, steamed

Wash and pick over beans and soak overnight in large pot with water to cover. Can use quick-soak method by covering beans with water and simmering for 2 hours or until beans are soft.

Drain beans and return to pot. Add 11/2 quarts cold water and bring to a boil. Crumble bacon into beans. Add garlic, onion, chili powder, cayenne, and salt. Add stock. Lower heat and simmer about 4 hours or until beans begin to fall apart. Sauce should not be rich and thick. Serve over steamed rice.

Serves 4

Beer Battered Chicken

2 or 3-pound fryer, cut up

seasoned flour:

1$^{1}/_{2}$ cups plain flour
1 teaspoon garlic salt
1$^{1}/_{2}$ teaspoons black pepper
1$^{1}/_{2}$ teaspoons paprika
$^{1}/_{4}$ teaspoon poultry seasoning

batter:

$^{2}/_{3}$ cup plain flour
$^{1}/_{2}$ teaspoon salt
$^{1}/_{8}$ teaspoon black pepper
1 beaten egg yolk
$^{3}/_{4}$ cup flat beer

Combine flour and seasonings in a medium bowl. For batter, combine egg yolk and beer (or water, if preferred). In another bowl, add dry ingredients. Heat Crisco shortening to 365 degrees in an electric skillet, deep pan, or deep fat fryer. Check temperature with deep fat thermometer. (Incidentally, a large, deep wok makes an excellent deep fat fryer.) Crisco should be about 2 inches deep.

Moisten chicken pieces. Dip in seasoned flour, then in batter, then back in seasoned flour. Fry in the hot Crisco for fifteen to twenty minutes until golden brown and well done, but be careful not to overcook. Drain on paper towels.

Serves 4-6

Shark Florida

2 pounds shark, cut into 2" chunks
3 tablespoons corn oil
1 large can pineapple chunks
1/4 cup cider vinegar
1/2 cup light brown sugar
3 tablespoons cornstarch
1 tablespoon soy sauce

1 teaspoon salt
1/8 teaspoon garlic powder
1 (8-ounce) can water chestnuts
1 cup green pepper squares
1 cut tomatoes, cut in thin wedges
1 cup pineapple juice
6 cups cooked rice

In a large skillet, sauté shark in oil for about five minutes. Drain pineapple and pour juice into a two-cup measuring cup. Mix liquid with cider vinegar, brown sugar, corn starch, soy sauce, and salt. Pour mix over shark and cook over medium heat. Add the rest of the ingredients and cook until vegetables are done. Cook five minutes longer.

Serve over rice with a sprinkle of soy sauce.

Serves 4

Baked Fish

"Use snapper, speckled trout (weakfish), and bass varieties. Other varieties of white-meat fish can be used in this recipe."

6 fish fillets, about 1/2 pound each
Pepper and salt, to taste
2 cups cream sauce (recipe below)
4 ounces mushrooms, chopped
5 egg yolks

1 tablespoon onion, finely chopped
1 tablespoon fresh parsley, minced
1/4 cup Parmesan cheese
1/2 teaspoon thyme
1/4 cup dry white wine

Season fish with pepper and a light amount of salt. Put them in a pot and boil for about five minutes. Remove; season with salt and pepper again.

Put fish in baking dish. With basic cream sauce, add other ingredients. Pour over the fish and bake at 325 degrees in preheated oven for about ten minutes. Check for doneness.

Serves 6

Béchamel (White or Cream Sauce)

"This sauce is quick and easy to prepare and has a score of possible uses. Creamed chicken or turkey, chipped beef, and macaroni and cheese (made by incorporating cheese into the sauce)."

> 1 tablespoon unsalted butter
> 1 tablespoon plain flour
> Salt and freshly ground pepper, to taste
> 1 cup liquid (whole milk, light cream, or clam broth)

Melt the butter and combine with flour in a small saucepan. Cook the two together until completely blended, stirring constantly. Stir in the liquid and stir constantly with a wire whisk until desired consistency is reached. If lumps appear, remove pan from heat and whisk the mixture until lumps are gone.

You can thicken this sauce by adding an extra tablespoon of both flour and butter while using the same amount of liquid as for the light sauce.

Makes approximately 1 cup

Grilled Shrimp

> $1/2$ pound large shrimp per person
> small mushroom caps

marinade:

> $1/2$ cup olive oil
> $1/3$ cup vinegar
> 1/2 cup orange juice
> $1/4$ cup onions,
>   finely chopped

> 3-4 drops Tabasco
> 1 teaspoon salt
> 1 teaspoon chili powder
> $1/4$ teaspoon oregano
> 1/4 tablespoon lemon juice

Prepare the seafood marinade by combining all of the ingredients. Peel and devein shrimp (large ones, $1/2$ pound per person to be served). Let the shrimp rest in the marinade for an hour or two. Thread the shrimp on skewers with a small mushroom cap between each and grill over a slow fire for about ten minutes. Baste with marinade occasionally while cooking.

Yield is variable

Tzatziki

"This is Helen Patronis' recipe for a traditional Greek favorite."

1 cucumber, pared and cubed
1 teaspoon salt
3/4 cup yogurt
1/2 cup dairy sour cream
1 small clove garlic, crushed

2 teaspoons onion, grated
1/2 teaspoon fresh lemon juice
1/4 teaspoon pepper
1/8 teaspoon red pepper sauce
1/2 teaspoon salt

Place cucumber in colander and sprinkle with 1 teaspoon salt. Let stand ten minutes. Rinse with cold water and drain on paper towels. Place cucumber in blender container or food processor. Blend on high speed until pureed, about two minutes. Place puree in colander; let stand six minutes. Mix yogurt and sour cream in a small bowl. Stir in garlic, onion, lemon juice, 1/2 teaspoon, pepper, and red pepper sauce. Stir in cucumber puree. Taste and adjust seasoning. Cover and place in refrigerator for at least four hours before serving, but no longer than 24 hours. Serve with crackers.

Makes approximately 2 1/2 cups

Cole Slaw

2 quarts cabbage, finely chopped
1 1/2 cups sour cream
2 egg yolks
2 tablespoons lemon juice

2 teaspoons prepared horseradish
1/4 teaspoon paprika
1 teaspoon sugar
1/2 teaspoon salt

In a food processor, chop the cabbage using the fine slicing blade. Combine sour cream and egg yolks in a bowl. Blend in other ingredients and pour the dressing over the cabbage. Toss to blend well, until all of the chopped cabbage is coated. Allow to marinate by refrigerating for at least a half hour before.

Makes approximately 2 1/2 quarts

Hush Puppies

*"The ultimate seafood accompaniment. Legend has it that many years ago,
people would toss scraps of fried cornbread to the dogs while giving the admonition 'hush puppy.'
Lucky dogs they were, to catch a mouthful of these southern treats."*

1 cup white cornmeal	$1/2$ cup onion, minced
$3/4$ cup plain flour	1 egg
2 teaspoons baking powder	$1/2$ cup buttermilk
$3/4$ teaspoons salt	3 tablespoons cooking oil

Sift dry ingredients in a bowl. Add other ingredients and blend well. Shape into small balls. Fry in deep fat until golden brown. Drain well on paper towels or brown paper.

Serves 6

Coconut Pie

3 large eggs	6 ounces shredded coconut
1 cup sugar	(either frozen or canned)
$1/4$ cup buttermilk	1 teaspoon vanilla extract
6 tablespoons unsalted butter,	Pinch of salt

Beat eggs and add sugar and buttermilk. To this mixture, add the melted butter and coconut. Add vanilla and salt. Bake in uncooked pie crust in preheated 350 degree oven for about ten minutes. Reduce heat to 300 degrees and bake for another thirty-five minutes. Check for doneness.

Makes 1 pie

Sweet Potato Pie

1 teaspoon powdered cloves	2 large eggs
1 teaspoon cinnamon	1^1/2 cups evaporated milk
^{1}/4 teaspoon nutmeg	1^1/2 cups sweet potatoes, boiled,
1 cup light brown sugar	peeled, and whipped smooth
^{1}/8 teaspoon salt	1 pie shell

Blend spices, sugar, and salt. Beat eggs with milk and combine with the sugar, spices, and sweet potatoes until smooth. In a saucepan, heat mixture until just before boiling point; pour mixture into an unbaked pie shell.

Bake in a preheated 400 degree oven for ten minutes. Reduce heat to 350 degrees and continue to bake until knife comes out clean, about 30 to 40 minutes. Top with whipped cream and serve.

Makes 1 pie

Coconut Candy

"Quick, easy, and tasty"

^{1}/2 loaf white sandwich bread
1 can Eagle Brand condensed milk
Sweetened Shredded Coconut

Cut the crust, from at least half or more slices of a loaf of sandwich bread. Cube the bread slices and place into an oblong glass baking dish. Pour the condensed milk over the bread cubes. Gently mix. Add a generous amount of shredded coconut. Reserve some of the coconut to spread over the top.

Put in a preheated 350 degree oven to toast the coconut. Cool and cut into squares. Do not over brown the coconut.

Barbecue Shrimp Parmesan   Gumbo Blanc
Greek Goat Ranch Salad Dressing

Captain Dave's on the Harbor

Destin, Florida

Dominating what is widely regarded as the Emerald Coast's favorite hangout -- the Destin Harbor -- Captain Dave's is not only the oldest seafood restaurant in town, it is also a complete "day full of Destin." For years, Captain Dave's has been serving the seafood that has made it a Destin tradition for both locals and visitors alike. On the menu you can find all of the traditional broiled, boiled, fried, and chargrilled seafood favorites, as well as some more unique combinations that have become house favorites. All these dishes are prepared by the twin brothers -- Chef Klaus and Chef Harold, who have been sending meals out of the galley almost as long as the galley has been there -- meals that keep Destin coming back for more.

The story of how Captain Dave's turned into a Destin tradition is no fish tale. Born with salt water in his veins, Capt. Dave Marler spent a dozen years plying the area waters as a charter boat captain before coming aground to open his restaurant. It was in the late 1800's, when there was only the Gulf, white sands, and sea oats around, Marler's grandfather, Billy Marler, found the fishing fine in local waters and told his friend Leonard Destin about it.

Twenty years ago, Capt. Dave decided he wanted to do more than pull those flapping snappers, groupers, and amberjacks out of the deep blue gulf waters. He wanted to find 'em, fillet 'em, and serve 'em up to hungry people, and so he opened Captain Dave's restaurant.

But, it hasn't always been smooth sailing for Captain Dave's. In 1975, Hurricane Eloise blasted through Destin. Capt. Dave, choosing to ride out the fierce storm, remembers watching his first oyster bar float down the harbor - looking much, as he said, like an overturned boat. A short time later, in 1979, another big one struck. (This time Hurricane Frederick.) Again, the Captain stayed with the "ship," standing on the chairs as the Gulf steadily rose in his restaurant. "But she took it like a champ" he said, noting the sturdy structure didn't even shake in the big winds.

Nowadays, Captain Dave's restaurant is stronger - and bigger - than ever. Visitors can watch Destin's fleet of boats arrive and depart from the cozy and colorful Dockside Cafe and bar. Or, if merely watching the boats proves to be a tease hop aboard one of Capt. Dave's private charters or the New Florida Girl, and head out into the aqua depths for a memorable fishing adventure. You can even scuba or snorkel your way to the whole other world that awaits you beneath the surface. Folks who prefer to stay dry can take a seat on the Glass Bottom Boat and watch the undersea world open beneath their feet. Of course, determined landlubbers can stroll the docks, bask in the sun, and browse through Captain Dave's Gift Shop. Whatever your idea of fun is, at Captain Dave's, you can enjoy yourself while the rest of the world floats by!

Barbecue Shrimp Parmesan

*"The recipes in this section were recently featured on local station
WEAR's production of Coastal Cooking."*

$1/4$ cup dried onion
2 teaspoons salt
3 pounds large shrimp
1 pound butter
$1/4$ cup olive oil
$1/4$ cup fresh garlic, minced

$1/2$ cup tomato paste
$1/2$ cup ketchup
1 dash Liquid Smoke
$1/2$ teaspoon Cavender's Greek Seasoning
$1/8$ teaspoon Zatarain's Crab Boil (liquid)
$1/2$ cup Parmesan, grated

Preheat oven to 450 degrees. Coat baking pan or large iron skillet with dried onion and salt. Arrange shrimp (single layer) on top of onion. In a separate skillet, heat butter and oil and sauté garlic for one minute. Add all other ingredients, except Parmesan. Pour this mixture over shrimp and bake until bubbly in middle. Dust with Parmesan and serve with French bread.

Serves 4-6

Gumbo Blanc

1 cup butter
1 cup flour
1 quart milk
1 pint half & half
2 tablespoons chicken base
1 quart boiling water
1 teaspoon garlic powder
1+ teaspoon salt
1 teaspoon black or white pepper

2 tablespoons dried onion
$1/2$ teaspoon dried mint
1 teaspoon Cavender's Greek seasoning
1 teaspoon dried parsley
$1/2$ pound crab claw meat
$1/2$ pound scallops
$1/2$ pound small peeled shrimp
$1/2$ cup Parmesan, grated

Stirring constantly, heat butter and flour in a saucepan over medium-high heat until smooth. Add milk, half & half, chicken base combined with hot water, and all spices. Whip until smooth. Add all seafood and heat on medium until shrimp is 90% cooked. Add parmesan and blend well. After all dried items have rehydrated, adjust to desired consistency with water or milk.

Makes approximately 1 gallon

Greek Goat Ranch Salad Dressing

"This dressing is so popular that it is scheduled to be Captain Dave's "signature" house dressing for 1995."

1 cup buttermilk
1 cup Kraft mayonnaise
1 tablespoon Cavender's Greek
   Seasoning

1 tablespoon dried onion
1 teaspoon dried parsley
$1/2$ cup feta cheese, crumbled
$1/2$ cup Parmesan, grated

Whip all ingredients using a wire whisk and chill.

Makes approximately 3 cups

Criolla Paella   Par Cooked Rice   Sofrito   Chaurice Sausage
Pan-Seared Soft Shell Crab Po Boy with Chayote Choux Choux
Kiss Yo' Mama Soup   Souffle Cornbread

Criolla's

Grayton Beach, Florida

A tour along scenic highway 30-A grants ample views of natural beauty to last anyone a lifetime. Running parallel to some of the Emerald Coast's more divine stretches of beaches, highway 30-A gives rise to other scenic wonders like the communities of Seaside and Grayton Beach, not to mention Johnny Earles' roadside Caribbean masterpiece, Criolla's restaurant. Arising from a stately cluster of banana and palm trees, Criolla's alluring and seductive facade captures both the eyes and the imaginations of the people who pass by. However, the real magic of Criolla's occurs within, where owner and chef Johnny Earles and his staff prepare the world's most superb Creole cuisine.

That Criolla's has won *Florida Trend* magazine's Golden Spoon Award since 1991, ranking it as one of Florida's top 20 restaurants, is by itself enough to describe the unsurpassed quality of Criolla's food and service. Couple these awards with Criolla's lush tropical atmosphere and its Caribbean motif and you have an enchanting restaurant that has set Florida ablaze with praise.

Criolla's success can be attributed largely to Mr. Earles' exceptional background. Mr. Earles grew up in southern Louisiana, the vortex of Creole culture in America, where he worked in restaurants since the age of fourteen. After leaving his native soil, Mr. Earles traveled the Caribbean islands, further expanding his knowledge of the ingredients, recipes, and preparation techniques that give Creole cuisine its unique flavor. After returning to the U.S., Mr. Earles settled in Grayton Beach, where he opened the Paradise Cafe at age 22. Although the restaurant was a hit from its inception, Mr. Earles eventually moved on to bigger and brighter things -- the founding of Criolla's restaurant. Today, Mr. Earles is still one of the busiest chefs around. Although in the warmer months he can be found in the kitchen preparing the dishes that have made Criolla's famous, in the off-season he works with some of the world's most renown restaurants and chefs, from New York to the Caribbean to the Basque region of Spain. Internationally influenced, Criolla's cuisine is, like Creole culture itself, a coalescence of different conventions and cultures. The Emerald Coast is truly lucky to have Criolla's as an integral part of the local landscape, and its unique spirit is ample cause for all of us here to celebrate.

Criolla Paella

"This recipe, recently published in Cooks Illustrated Magazine, is a simplified version of a notoriously difficult dish, yet especially delicious."

Note: When expanding the recipe, the amount of liquid used to par cook the rice must be reduced by 20 percent. Everything else multiplies out correctly. Recipes for two or more may be cooked together in a larger pan.

^{3}/4 cup boneless skinless chicken thighs
Chili powder, to taste
Olive oil
^{3}/4 cup sofrito (recipe below)
4 ounces chicken stock
5 strands saffron
^{1}/2 ounce white wine
1^1/2 cups par cooked arborio rice
   (recipe below)
^{1}/2 cup blanched lady peas
   (white peas, field peas)

^{1}/2 cup chaurice sausage (recipe below)
   or chorizo sausage, cooked
2 ounces rock shrimp, peeled deveined
3 ounces fresh squid, cleaned and sliced
   into ^{1}/4 inch rings
8 fresh mussels, cleaned and de-bearded
2 ounces lobster knuckles
1 scallion, chopped
Salt, to taste
1 tablespoon fresh cilantro
   (coriander), chopped

Preheat oven to 450 degrees. Dust the boneless chicken thighs with the chili powder. In a large skillet on medium-high heat, add the olive oil and sear the chicken on both sides until just done. Remove from skillet. (The chicken may be refrigerated up to 48 hours in advance.)

In an 8-inch paella pan, bring the sofrito, chicken stock, saffron, and white wine to a slow boil. Add the par cooked rice, peas, chicken, and sausage. Cook for 2 minutes. Add all seafood, except the mussels, the scallion and salt. Place uncovered in oven 5-6 minutes. Arrange mussels in a circle in the paella so that when opened they will stand above the rest of the paella. Return to oven for another 5 minutes. Remove and cover with foil. Allow to stand for 10 minutes before serving. Garnish with chopped cilantro.

Par Cooked Rice

1^1/2 cups rich chicken stock
2 tablespoons olive oil
1 cup raw arborio rice

In a small sauce pot, bring the chicken stock to a gentle boil. In a large skillet, heat the olive oil to just before smoking and add rice. Stir constantly for 60 seconds and slowly add the heated chicken stock. Quickly bring to a boil, stirring constantly for 3 minutes. Remove from the heat and allow the rice to absorb the chicken stock. Spread the par cooked rice onto a cookie sheet and place flat in a cooler. Save until paella assembly. Will keep for 2-3 days if covered and refrigerated.

Sofrito

"A Latin tradition with Spanish, Cuban, and Puerto Rican influences. It was conceived by cooks who wanted to capture and preserve the fresh seasonal qualities of the vegetables for use in the off-season."

4 cups yellow onion, diced medium
2 teaspoons garlic, chopped
1 cup poblano chile, roasted, peeled, deseeded, and diced
¹/4 cup olive oil

4 bay leaves
3 cups Roma tomato, skinned, seedless, and chopped
1 tablespoon fresh oregano, chopped
¹/4 cup fresh cilantro, chopped
2 tablespoons sugar

In a large non-reactive skillet, sauté the onions, garlic, and poblano in olive oil until the onions are translucent. Add remaining ingredients and simmer for 25 minutes. Remove from heat. Let mixture cool and refrigerate. Will keep refrigerated for two weeks and can be used as a starter for many dishes, including black beans, chili, and soup.

Chaurice Sausage

"A traditional New Orleans Creole sausage. Very spicy! The cinnamon gives it an exceptional twist."

5 pounds pork, veal, or rabbit, ground
2 cups yellow onion, brunoise
1¹/4 cups fresh parsley, chopped
3 tablespoons garlic, chopped
1 tablespoon cayenne pepper
1 tablespoon black pepper
2 teaspoons white pepper
2 teaspoons thyme

1¹/2 teaspoons nutmeg
³/4 teaspoon cinnamon
1 tablespoon kosher salt
1 tablespoon coriander
1 tablespoon cumin
1 tablespoon olive oil
1 teaspoon chile powder (ancho, chimayo, etc.)

Mix all ingredients in a non-reactive bowl and pipe into casings, make into patties, or roll into one-inch meat balls.

If in casings, place sausage into a baking pan at least 2 inches deep with ¹/2 inch of water. Place in a 375 degree oven for approximately 25 minutes; inside temperature must reach 165 degrees. Remove from oven and allow to cool. Remove chaurice from water bath and refrigerate. Slice into one inch lengths.

If in half-inch patties, cook in a pan on medium heat for 5 minutes on each side until done.

If in meatballs, place on a sheet pan in a 375 degree oven for 20 minutes.

Pan Seared Soft Shell Crab Po Boy with Chayote Choux Choux

"When Seafood Magazine requested a dish that was intense in flavor but also light, Chef Earles created this. The choux choux is an easy relish to make and it stays fresh for a long time. It's worth waiting for fresh crabs, which are becoming increasingly available in supermarkets nationwide. Frozen crabs and refrigerated crab meat can greatly diminish the quality of this dish."

Chayote Choux Choux

1 cup cabbage, finely chopped
$3/4$ cup chayote (mirliton) squash, peeled, seeded, and diced chayote or same amount of cauliflower, chopped
$1/2$ cup onion, chopped
$1/2$ cup green bell pepper, diced
$1/4$ cup red bell pepper, chopped
$1/4$ cup green tomatoes, chopped
$1/4$ cup carrot, julienned

1 tablespoon jalapeno peppers, minced
1 tablespoon salt
$2/3$ cup distilled white vinegar
3 tablespoons sugar
$1/2$ teaspoon celery seed
$1/2$ teaspoon dry mustard or 1/4 teaspoon mustard seed
$1/4$ teaspoon turmeric
$1/8$ teaspoon dry ground ginger

Combine cabbage, chayote, onion, bell peppers, tomatoes, carrot and jalapeno in a bowl; toss with salt and let stand 5 to 6 hours or overnight at room temperature. Drain vegetables.

In large non-aluminum pan, combine the vinegar, sugar, celery seed, mustard, turmeric, and ginger. Cover and simmer for 10 minutes. Add vegetables. Cover and simmer, stirring occasionally, until vegetables are tender-crisp, 15 to 20 minutes.

Cool choux choux and store it in a tightly covered container in the refrigerator for up to 1 month.

Soft Shell Crab

1 fresh soft blue crab, cleaned
Chili powder, such as Chimayo or Ancho
Kosher salt
1 ounce peanut oil

Heat a skillet to medium high heat. Lightly dust bottom side of crab with chili powder and salt. Sauté with bottom side down in 1 ounce peanut oil for $1^1/2$ minutes. Turn and sauté for $1^1/2$ minutes more and remove.

Place 2 tablespoons choux choux on sour dough toast and put crab on top.

Kiss Yo' Mama Soup

"An outstanding dish from South Louisiana. Named as such because it's so good, it makes you want to "kiss yo' mama." Chef Earles strongly recommends that you hold out for fresh crawfish tails. The difference they make is outstanding."

2 cups yellow onion, chopped
14 cups fresh corn, cut off the cob
　　(substitute frozen corn only)
4 medium-size chipotle chiles, chopped
　　(substitute canned chipotles, if necessary)
1 cup poblano chiles, roasted, peeled,
　　chopped (substitute canned green chiles)
1/2 pound butter, unsalted

2 cups chicken stock
6 cups milk
Salt, to taste
1 pound sour cream
1 pound Louisiana crawfish tails
1/2 cup fresh goat cheese
　　(such as Chevre)
1/4 cup fresh chives, chopped

In a non-reactive pot, sauté the onion, corn, chipotles, and poblanos in 1/2 pound of butter over medium heat for 5 minutes. Add chicken stock. Cover and simmer for 15 minutes. Remove from heat and cool for 15 minutes. Puree mixture in a blender or food processor and strain through a medium sieve using a rubber spatula in order to retrieve as much as possible. Discard pulp. Add milk and return to the non-reactive pot and slowly bring to a boil. Reduce heat to a simmer for 5 minutes, stirring frequently. Season with salt to taste. Remove from heat and stir in the sour cream and crawfish tails. Salt to taste. Garnish with dollops of goat cheese and chopped chives and serve.

Makes 1 1/2 gallons

Soufflé Cornbread

"Chef Earles created this dish because he felt that standard cornbread needed a kick. Corn juice intensifies the flavor of this bread; the egg whites make it lighter; and the absence of the usual buttermilk makes it healthier."

4 eggs, separated
6 ounces butter
2 1/4 cups corn juice
1 cup cream
3 cups corn meal

1 tablespoon salt
2 tablespoons baking powder
2 cups all purpose flour
1/2 cup + 2 tablespoons sugar
Chiles (optional)
Colored bell peppers (optional)

Blend egg yolks with butter. Add corn juice and cream. Mix for 5 minutes. In a mixing bowl, blend dry ingredients. Fold wet ingredients into dry mixture, incorporating optional ingredients at this time. In a mixer bowl, whip whites to medium peaks and fold in. Place in buttered soufflé dish and bake at 350 degrees for 13 minutes or until knife inserted in middle comes out clean.

Grilled Chicken Breast with Stone Ground Mustard and Herbs   Pasta Mediterranean
Grouper Elizabeth   Seafood Alfredo   Pasta Sitka   Gumbo   Chilled Plum Soup
Lobster Bisque   Crab Cakes   Poppyseed Vinaigrette   Chicken Stock   Seafood Cream
Sauce   Butter Sauce   Crabmeat Hozel   Elephant Walk Salad   Cajun Spice
Chocolate Decadence with Raspberry Sauce

Elephant Walk

Sandestin, Florida

The legend of Elephant Walk's success begins with an historical misfortune. Back in 1890, John Wiley took cover while a herd of elephants trampled his father's tea plantation in Ceylon. Emerging from the ruins of the devastated plantation, Wiley set out to start anew and wandered the world for thirty years. Eventually landing on the shores of Florida, Wiley knew when he discovered the beaches of Sandestin that he had found his new home. And, indeed, this is where he began construction of the Elephant Walk Restaurant.

Today, the restaurant commemorates the treasures that Wiley found during his long journey to Sandestin, including dishes like Tahitianese Duck, Shrimp and Lobster Ragout, and Tamarind Tango Tuna. These culinary delights, collected from Wiley's wanderings around the world, are brought together and served in one of the Emerald Coast's most spectacular restaurants. The Elephant Walk is an architectural wonder rising above the brilliant white dunes and the aqua waters of the sun-splashed Gulf of Mexico.

In this colorful jungle setting, guests have their choice of a wide variety of dishes ranging from seafood favorites and international gourmet fare to more traditional dishes. This award-winning cuisine has led *Florida Trend* magazine to rank Elephant Walk as one of Florida's top 200 restaurants and has made it winner of the Emerald Coast Chef's Challenge.

Visitors to the Elephant Walk can explore their taste buds with the white sands and Gulf of Mexico as a backdrop to an evening of adventure. A visit to the Elephant Walk, with its splendid cuisine and its dazzling South Asian motif all aglow under a radiant sunset, promises to be an evening of pure enchantment.

Grilled Chicken Breast with
Stone Ground Mustard and Herbs

"This dish is a traditional favorite known around the country."

2 (5-ounce) boneless chicken
   breasts (with skin)
Salt and pepper, to taste
1 ounce salad oil
2 ounces white wine

4 ounces heavy whipping cream
2 ounces stone ground mustard
$1/2$ teaspoon fresh thyme, chopped
$1/4$ teaspoon fresh tarragon, chopped

Season chicken skin with salt and pepper. Heat 1 ounce salad oil in sauté pan until smoking. Place chicken skin side down in pan and brown. When skin is browned, turn chicken over and place in a 300 degree oven until done. When the chicken is cooked, remove from pan and discard grease. Deglaze pan with white wine and reduce liquid. Add heavy whipping cream, mustard, and herbs, and reduce to desired consistency. Salt and pepper to taste.

Serves 2

Pasta Mediterranean

$1/4$ cup of extra virgin olive oil
1 large zucchini, diced to 1/2-inch
$1^1/2$ pounds fresh mushrooms
4 cloves garlic, minced
1 cup tomato juice

$1/2$ pound fresh spinach, shredded to 1-inch
$1/2$ cup sundried tomatoes, diced to $1/4$-inch
5 large tomatoes, diced to $1/2$-inch
Salt and pepper, to taste
Pasta, any shape, cooked

"This is Elephant Walk's version of a Tunisian favorite."

Add olive oil to a large sauté pan and place over medium heat. Add zucchini, mushrooms, and garlic, and sauté until tender. Add tomato juice, spinach, and sundried tomatoes. Simmer for 5 minutes. Add fresh chopped tomatoes and simmer for 2 minutes. Season with salt and pepper to taste. Pour over cooked pasta and top with your favorite cheese.

Serves 4

Grouper Elizabeth

"Words cannot describe this house favorite."

2 teaspoons clarified butter
4 (8-ounce) grouper filets
Salt and pepper, to taste
$^1/_4$ cup white wine or butter stock
12 ounces Elephant Walk Butter
   Sauce (recipe in this section)

$^1/_4$ cup fresh chives, chopped
$^1/_2$ cup peeled tomatoes,
   diced to $^1/_2$ inch
$^1/_2$ pound jumbo lump crab meat
$^1/_4$ cup toasted sliced almonds

Preheat oven to 400 degrees. Heat butter in a large sauté pan until smoking point and reserve. Season the grouper with salt and pepper. Place fish in hot butter skin side up and cook until golden brown. Flip fish and deglaze with wine or butter stock. Place in oven for 20 minutes. Heat the butter sauce. Add chives, tomatoes, and crab meat. Arrange the cooked fish on a platter and top with the sauce. Sprinkle with almonds.

Serves 4

Seafood Alfredo

"A rich, creamy favorite imported from Southern Italy."

2 pounds gulf shrimp,
   peeled and deveined
1 pound sea scallops
Salt and white pepper, to taste
1 quart Elephant Walk
   Seafood Cream Sauce
   (recipe in this section)

1 carrot, julienned
1 green zucchini, julienned
2 tablespoons fresh tarragon, chopped
$^1/_2$ cup grated Romano cheese
1 pound jumbo lump crab meat, cooked
1 pound of favorite pasta,
   cooked al dente and hot

Season shrimp and scallops lightly with salt and white pepper. In a large sauté pan, bring the Seafood Cream sauce to a simmer on medium heat. Add the scallops and simmer until cooked through 50%, then add the shrimp. When shrimp are almost cooked through, add carrots, zucchini, tarragon, and Romano cheese. Simmer for a few minutes. Add jumbo lump crab meat and mix well. Adjust seasonings and spoon off in a platter over favorite pasta.

Serves 8

Pasta Sitka

"Smoked salmon in a seafood cream sauce."

1/2 pound cooked penne pasta
2 cups Elephant Walk Seafood Cream
   Sauce (recipe in this section)
1/4 pound smoked salmon, diced

1 teaspoon fresh dill, chopped
3 sprigs fresh dill
1 tomato, peeled, seeded,
   and diced to 1/2 inch

Cook pasta al dente. Heat Seafood Cream Sauce in a large sauté pan. Add smoked salmon and simmer for 4 minutes. Add chopped dill and pasta and toss them in the simmering sauce. Reduce until sauce nicely coats pasta. Place pasta on a serving plate and garnish with dill and diced tomato.
Serves 3

Elephant Walk Gumbo

"Spicy crawfish and shrimp submerged in a hearty clam velout."

1/2 pound bacon, diced
1 medium onion
1 medium red bell pepper
1 medium green bell pepper
6 ounces margarine, melted
1 1/2 cups flour
1/2 cup paprika
1/2 gallon clam juice
1 ounce Worcestershire

1/2 tablespoon gumbo file
1/2 tablespoon thyme
1/2 tablespoon basil
1/2 tablespoon oregano
1/4 teaspoon each white and black pepper
1 teaspoon cayenne pepper
13 ounces heavy whipping cream
2 pounds small shrimp, peeled and cooked
3/4 pound crawfish tails, cooked

Cook bacon until crisp. Add vegetables and sauté. Add flour, paprika, and margarine. Stir until a tight roux develops. Add clam juice, stirring constantly. Add all other ingredients except for last three items. Simmer approximately one hour, whisking every 5 to 10 minutes. Cream, shrimp, and crawfish tails must be added to the gumbo at time of serving.

Chilled Plum Soup

"This soup makes a great summer appetizer."

2 teaspoons granulated sugar	1 tablespoon ground cinnamon
6 teaspoons bourbon whiskey	1/2 cup fresh orange juice
4 cups canned pitted plums in syrup	1/2 cup nonfat yogurt
4 teaspoons honey	12 thin slices fresh plums
2 cups milk	Orange zest
	6 fresh mint sprigs

Place sugar in a non-stick skillet over medium heat and caramelize. Add bourbon. Remove from heat and set aside. Place plums, honey, milk, cinnamon, orange juice, and yogurt in a blender. Puree until smooth. Add bourbon and sugar mixture to blender. Blend until smooth. Refrigerate in a plastic container. To serve, ladle into chilled bowls with plums, mint, and orange zest.

Serves 2

Lobster Bisque

1/2 cup olive oil	4 ripe tomatoes
2 live Maine Lobsters	1 tablespoon dried tarragon
1 onion, diced to 2"	1 (46-ounce) can clam juice
2 carrots, diced to 2"	2 cups dry white wine
3 ribs of celery, diced to 2"	1/4 cup tomato paste
3 garlic cloves	1/2 cup brandy
1 pound butter	Heavy cream, as needed
1 1/2 cups flour	Salt and pepper, to taste

In a wide, heavy pot, add olive oil and put on medium heat. Dice lobster into 2-inch pieces and add to oil. Sauté for 5 minutes. Add onion, carrot, celery, and garlic. Sauté until vegetables are tender. Add 1 pound butter and melt. Add flour and cook for 10 minutes. Add tomatoes, tarragon, clam juice, white wine, and tomato paste. Simmer for 1/2 hour. Strain all ingredients, saving liquid. Return strained liquid to pot and add brandy. Simmer for 5 minutes. Add heavy cream and stir to desired consistency. Season with salt and pepper.

Makes 2 quarts

Crab Cakes

"An award-winning recipe from the shores of the Chesapeake Bay."

3 tablespoons mayonnaise
1 tablespoon Dijon mustard
1 teaspoon dry mustard
1 whole egg
1 egg yolk
$1/4$ teaspoon celery seed
3 dashes Worcestershire sauce
2-3 dashes Tabasco sauce
Juice of $1/2$ fresh lemon
2 tablespoons Old Bay seasoning

3 tablespoons chopped parsley
4 tablespoons chopped pimento
3 tablespoons scallions, chopped
1 pound jumbo lump crab meat
$1/2$ pound crab claw meat
Fine bread crumbs
    (enough to bind ingredients)
Small diced bread
    (enough to bind ingredients)

Combine all ingredients except bread, bread crumbs, crab meat, and claw meat. Mix thoroughly. Add crab meat and claw meat and mix. Add bread crumbs and diced bread until the mixture coheres well. Form mixture into cakes and dust with fine bread crumbs. Sauté cakes in butter or deep fry. The crab cakes can be frozen in their raw state.

Makes 12 ($1^1/2$ ounce) cakes

Poppyseed Vinaigrette

"A popular accompaniment to any mixed greens or fruit salad."

$3/8$ gallon water
1 cup sugar
1 cup juice of fresh lemons
$3/8$ cup juice of fresh limes
$1/2$ cup juice of fresh oranges
1 tablespoon orange juice
    concentrate

1 shallot, finely diced
8 raspberries, smashed
1 tablespoon Grenadine
$1/8$ cup red wine vinegar
$1^3/4$ cups vegetable oil
$1/2$ cup poppy seeds
Salt and pepper, to taste

Boil water with sugar. Combine all ingredients, except vegetable oil and poppy seeds, and add to the sugar mixture. Slowly add vegetable oil while blending. Season to taste. Add poppy seeds at serving time.

Makes approximately 3 quarts

Chicken Stock

3 pounds chicken necks and backs
1 large onion
2 carrots, peeled and thickly
   chopped
1 leek, chopped
2 ribs celery, washed and chopped

1 bay leaf
2 cloves garlic
$^{1}/_{4}$ teaspoon thyme
3 parsley sprigs

Spread chicken parts on a baking tin and roast in a 400 degree oven for 30 minutes or until browned. Transfer them to a large, heavy soup kettle. Brown all of the vegetables in the baking tin over medium heat and add to the chicken parts. Add 2 cups water to the baking tin and bring to a boil, scraping up all the brown bits and adding them to the soup kettle with enough cold water to cover the bones and vegetables. Bring to a boil and skim. Add the rest of the ingredients and simmer over low heat 4 to 5 hours. Remove mixture from heat and let stand uncovered for $^{1}/_{2}$ hour, allowing sediment to settle. Strain through a cheesecloth lined strainer. Refrigerate in a plastic container.

Makes 3 gallons

Seafood Cream Sauce

"This sauce is excellent with any seafood, seafood pastas, etc., and can be flavored with any herbs or spices."

46 ounces clam juice
1 cup dry white wine
6 shallots
1$^{1}/_{2}$ quarts heavy cream

Place clam juice, white wine, and shallots in a large sauté pan. Simmer until reduced 70%. Add heavy cream and reduce to half.

Makes 1 quart

Butter Sauce

1/4 cup olive oil
5 shallots
1 head garlic, roughly chopped
1 head of fresh fennel, roughly
  chopped
1/2 Bermuda onion, roughly chopped

1 gallon dry white wine
1 ounce fresh tarragon, roughly
  chopped
1 1/2 pounds unsalted butter, cubed
Salt and pepper, to taste

In a deep soup or stock pot, heat olive oil and sauté all dry ingredients under cover on low heat until all vegetables are translucent and tender, not brown.

Add wine and simmer for 20 minutes. Strain off ingredients, keeping liquid for future use. Heat 1 cup of the strained liquid. Cut 1 1/2 pounds unsalted butter in cubes and add 1/2 of the cubed butter to the hot liquid, whisking constantly. Remove from heat. Add remaining cubed butter to liquid until incorporated. Mix with a hand-mixer for 2 minutes. Season with salt and pepper.

Makes 1 gallon

Crab Meat Hozel

"The Emerald Coast's finest crab meat cocktail."

8 shallots, finely minced
2 tablespoons fresh tarragon,
  finely chopped
1/4 cup fresh lemon juice
1/2 cup vegetable oil

1 tablespoon fresh parsley, finely
  chopped
Salt, to taste
White pepper, to taste
1 pound fresh jumbo lump crab meat
8 red leaf lettuce leaves

Combine the shallots, tarragon, lemon juice, oil, and parsley and season with salt and white pepper. Add the crab meat to the seasoned salad dressing. On four salad plates, arrange red lettuce leaves to form a cup. Divide the crab meat salad into fourths and place on lettuce.

Serves 4

Elephant Walk Salad

"A great complement to any meal."

4 large ripe tomatoes,
   sliced $1/2$-inch thick
15 shallots, peeled and sliced
1 cup feta cheese, crumbled
20 slices crisp cooked bacon,
   crumbled

$1/2$ cup fresh basil, chopped
Olive oil
Balsamic vinegar
Sea salt, to taste
Cracked black pepper, to taste

Arrange sliced tomatoes on 4 plates. Top with sliced shallots, feta cheese, bacon, and fresh basil. Sprinkle with salt and pepper. Top with 3 parts oil and 1 part balsamic vinegar.

Serves 4

Cajun Spice

"A secret blend of herbs and spices made exclusively by Elephant Walk. Use this spice on any kind of meat, fish, or poultry for outstanding results."

1 cup paprika
$7/8$ cup salt
$1 1/4$ cups sugar
$1/2$ cup thyme
$1/2$ cup basil
$1/2$ cup oregano

$3/4$ cup granulated garlic
$1/4$ cup onion powder
$1/8$ cup cayenne pepper
$1/8$ cup white pepper
$1/4$ cup dry mustard
$1/8$ cup black pepper

Thoroughly mix all ingredients. Keep in an airtight container in spice cabinet. Recipe can easily be halved or quartered.

To use: dust product with desired amount of spice. Rub lightly with salad oil, then place on hot cooking surface (either in a sauté pan or on a grill).

Makes $6 1/2$ cups

Chocolate Decadence with Raspberry Sauce

"A delicious desert requested by Gourmet Magazine."

$5^1/3$ ounces unsalted butter $^1/4$ cup flour
$5^1/3$ ounces lightly salted butter $^1/4$ cup sugar
$3^2/3$ pounds semisweet chocolate   14 eggs

Heat butter and chocolate over water bath until melted. Sift flour into chocolate and incorporate until smooth. In a separate bowl, add sugar to eggs and mix. Add egg mixture to chocolate mixture. Mix on low speed about 5 minutes. Bake at 250 degrees for 10 minutes. Cake should bake only $1^1/2$ inches high. Top with Raspberry Sauce.

Raspberry Sauce

2 pints fresh raspberries
Juice of $^1/2$ fresh lemon
4 tablespoons corn syrup

Push berries through a fine sieve into bowl. Discard the pulp and seeds. Warm corn syrup and lemon juice in a sauce pan to 110 degrees. Stir warm corn syrup into raspberry puree and mix well. Place in refrigerator until ready to use.

Makes 1 cake

Ingredients and Cooking Terms

Cavender's Greek Seasoning: another commercially available blend of spices. You should not have any trouble finding it at your grocery.

Chayote: A squash-like vegetable that is wildly popular in South Louisiana and more particularly in New Orleans, where it is more commonly called mirliton. You can usually find it in markets that specialize in South American and West Indies imports and in some of the more trend-setting grocery chains. If you never tried it before, get ready for a new favorite.

Clarified butter: When butter is heated it separates into two parts: a clear, yellow liquid and a more opaque group of milk solids. The clear liquid, when drawn away from the sediment, is called clarified butter.

Deglaze: a French term widely used in cooking. When you saute' or roast food in butter or oil, you will often find that a lot of juices develop and gradually begin to form a "glaze" on the bottom of the pan. Since this residue contains a lot of flavor, it is usually desirable to preserve it by incorporating it into the dish or sauce once the fatty liquids have been drained. You do this by adding wine or broth to the skillet, which loosens and melts the residual glaze that has formed on the bottom of the pan during cooking and prevents it from being burned. Once the pan has been deglazed, a cream or broth is usually added to the sauce to make it even more flavorful.

File or File Powder: a powder made from dried sassafras leaves and used as a thickener and seasoning in Southern gumbos. If you cannot find commercial file, you can easily make it yourself by drying fresh sassafras leaves in your microwave and then grinding them to a powder once they have turned crisp.

More tips on page 57.

Snapper Destin   Soft-shell Crawfish on Eggplant
Corn and Crab Chowder   Mystery Pie

Flamingo Cafe

Destin, Florida

Destin's most exquisite waterfront restaurant, the immensely popular Flamingo Cafe mixes the casual atmosphere of a cafe with the style and quality of a gourmet restaurant. Along with our Cajun influenced continental cuisine, come and savor Chef Jim Richard's "Floribbean Cuisine" -- an innovative international island fare introducing fresh Florida seafood to a unique blend of tropical fruit and Caribbean flavors. Sound delicious? *Florida Trend* magazine thought so when it ranked Flamingo Cafe as one of the Top 200 restaurants in Florida.

Flamingo Cafe artfully matches its prized cuisine with an equally captivating setting; the restaurant rises above the waterfront with its alluring pink and white Caribbean facade, commanding a truly arresting view of the Destin Harbor -- the bustling point of departure and return for Florida's busiest (and luckiest) fishing fleets. For a closer look, visitors can dine on the full length outdoor veranda, which from the harbor appears to be suspended over a cluster of wild palms. Few other restaurants achieve such an intriguing style, and fewer still successfully combine a resplendent atmosphere with such splendid cuisine like Flamingo Cafe.

Dining at Flamingo Cafe, you will realize that it is literally impossible to get any closer to the Emerald Coast's freshest seafood. Flamingo Cafe house specialties include Oysters Bienville, Snapper Destin, Grouper Ponchartrain, Triggerfish Napoleon, and Potato Crusted Bay Redfish. When in Destin, visit the Flamingo Cafe, the only place where the Emerald Coast touches the Caribbean

Snapper Destin

This is our most requested dish on the menu, year in, year out!"

1 tablespoon sea salt
2 teaspoons paprika
1 teaspoon black pepper
1 teaspoon white pepper
1/2 teaspoon cayenne pepper
1 teaspoon garlic powder
2 pounds red snapper fillets
  (cut into 4 to 6 pieces)
1/4 cup butter or margarine, melted

8-12 peeled jumbo fresh shrimp, peeled
  and deveined, tails on
1 pound fresh lump crab meat,
  picked and cleaned
1/2 cup Hollandaise Sauce (recipe in this section)
1/2 cup Lemon Meuniere sauce
  (recipe in this section)
1/2 cup Garlic Beurre Blanc sauce
  (recipe in this section)

Combine all seasonings. Rub fillets with melted butter and season to taste with the seasonings. Grill over medium-high heat 3-5 minutes on each side or until fish flakes easily when tested with a fork.

Sauté the shrimp and crab meat in remaining butter, adding if necessary. Season to taste.

Spoon 2 tablespoons of each sauce onto each plate. Place fillet on sauces. Top each fillet with 1/4 cup crab meat and 2 shrimp. If desired, garnish with lemon wedges and scallions.

Serves 4-6

Soft-shell Crawfish on Eggplant

"Flamingo Cafe's signature appetizer. Also featured in Southern Living magazine."

20 whole soft-shell crawfish
  (about 3/4 pound)
1 cup all-purpose flour
2 tablespoons paprika
1 tablespoon black pepper
1 tablespoon white pepper
1 1/2 teaspoons crushed red pepper
1 1/2 teaspoons garlic powder
1 egg, slightly beaten

1/2 cup milk
4 slices eggplant approximately 3/4" thick
Vegetable oil
1/2 cup Hollandaise sauce
  (recipe in this section)
1/2 cup Lemon Meuniere (recipe in this section)
1/2 cup Garlic Beurre Blanc sauce
  (recipe in this section)
3/4 cup Glazed Nuts (recipe in this section)

Prepare crawfish by removing the heads, including small ball, but leaving shells and tails intact. Set aside. Combine flour and next 5 ingredients; set aside. In a separate bowl, combine egg and milk and stir well.

Dip eggplant slices into egg mixture and then dredge them in flour mixture. Pour oil to depth of 1 inch in a heavy saucepan and heat to 350 degrees. Fry eggplant 2 to 3 minutes or until golden brown. Drain on paper towels.

Dip crawfish in egg mixture and then dredge them in flour mixture. Pour oil to depth of 1 inch in a heavy saucepan and heat to 350 degrees. Fry crawfish about 2 minutes or until shells are bright in color and batter is golden brown. Drain on paper towels. (continued)

Spoon 2 tablespoons of each sauce onto each serving plate. Place a slice of eggplant in the center of the plate and top with 5 crawfish. Sprinkle 3 tablespoons of Glazed Nuts over crawfish. Garnish with lemon wedges.

Makes 4 appetizer servings

Hollandaise Sauce

> **6 egg yolks**
> **1 tablespoon dry white wine**
> **2 tablespoons lemon juice**
> **1^1/2 cups melted butter**

Combine egg yolks, wine, and lemon juice in the top of a double boiler. Place over boiling water, and cook, beating at medium speed of an electric mixer, 3 minutes or until thickened. Remove from heat. Add butter, one tablespoon at a time, beating at medium speed until thickened.

Makes 2 cups

Lemon Meuniere Sauce

> **3 tablespoons lemon juice**
> **2 tablespoons white wine**
> **1 tablespoon white vinegar**
> **1 shallot, chopped**

> **^{1}/4 cup+2 tablespoons whipping cream**
> **2 cups butter, softened**
> **1 tablespoon veal reduction***
> **^{1}/2 teaspoon garlic, minced**

* Note: If you cannot use veal stock, either canned or fresh beef stock or bouillon may be substituted.

Combine first four ingredients in a saucepan; bring mixture to a boil. Boil 2 minutes or until 95% of liquid evaporates. Add whipping cream and bring to a boil. Boil for 1 minute. Remove from heat. Cool for 2 minutes. Return to low heat. Add butter, 2 tablespoons at a time, stirring with a whisk until butter is incorporated. Keep sauce temperature at 140 degrees. Stir in veal reduction and garlic. The sauce will separate if reheated.

Makes 2 cups

Garlic Beurre Blanc Sauce

> 2 tablespoons white wine
> 1 tablespoon white vinegar
> 6 cloves garlic, chopped
> 1 shallot, chopped
> 1/2 cup whipping cream
> 2 cups butter, softened

Combine first four ingredients in a saucepan; bring mixture to a boil. Boil 2 minutes or until 95% of liquid evaporates. Add whipping cream and heat until mixture comes to a boil again. Boil for 1 minute. Remove from heat and let cool for 2 minutes. Return to low heat. Add butter, 2 tablespoons at a time, stirring with a whisk until the butter is incorporated. Keep sauce temperature at 160 degrees. (The sauce will separate if reheated.)

Makes 2 cups

Glazed Nuts

> 3 3/4 cups pecan pieces
> 3 cups slivered almonds
> 1/2 cup sugar
> 1/2 teaspoon seasoned salt
> 1/4 cup vegetable oil

Combine all ingredients in a large heavy skillet. Cook over medium heat for approximately 5 minutes or until golden brown, stirring constantly. Immediately spread nuts in a thin layer on a jellyroll pan and cool. Stir occasionally to separate nuts.

Makes 6 3/4 cups

Corn and Crab Chowder

"This dish is a real crowd pleaser"

1-2 pounds crabmeat, cooked
1 red bell pepper, diced
1 green bell pepper, diced
1 yellow bell pepper, diced
1 medium onion, diced
4 stalks celery, diced
1 small can undrained cream style corn
1 small can undrained whole kernel corn
$^1/4$ teaspoon cayenne pepper

$1^1/2$ teaspoons black pepper
2 bay leaves
2 quarts chicken stock
2 cups roux (50/50 ratio fat to flour)
1 quart heavy whipping cream
$^3/4$ cup sugar
Salt, to taste
White pepper, to taste

In a stock pot, sauté peppers, onion, celery, and corn with cayenne, black pepper, and bay leaves. Add chicken stock and bring to a boil. Reduce heat to simmer and add roux. Let mixture simmer for 10 to 15 minutes. While stirring, gradually add heavy whipping cream. Stir in the sugar and add salt and pepper to taste. Add the desired amount of crab meat to the chowder at time of serving.

Serves 10

Mystery Pie

"So delicious, Gourmet Magazine requested this recipe."

8 ounces cream cheese
5 eggs
$1^1/2$ cups granulated sugar
1 tablespoon pure vanilla
$^3/4$ cup light corn syrup

$^1/4$ cup lightly salted butter, melted
$1^1/2$ cups medium chopped pecans
1 prepared pastry shell
Praline sauce (recipe next page)

In mixing bowl, using paddle, soften cream cheese until completely smooth. Make sure to periodically scrape bowl so that no lumps form. With mixer on low, add 2 eggs, one at a time, and incorporate thoroughly. Gradually add $^1/2$ cup of sugar and pure vanilla and mix well for 3 minutes. Place mixture in refrigerator.

In a separate bowl, whisk the 3 remaining eggs. Add 1 cup sugar, corn syrup, and melted butter. Fold in pecans.

Remove cream cheese mixture from refrigerator and lightly fold into pecan mixture, making a marbling effect. Pour into prepared pastry shell. Place into preheated oven and bake 70-80 minutes or until knife, inserted in the middle, comes out clean. Cool completely and then store in refrigerator.

Makes 1 (9-inch) pie which serves 6-8

Praline Sauce

$1/2$ cup granulated sugar
2 teaspoons brown sugar
$3/4$ cup heavy whipping cream (heated before boiling point)
1 teaspoon pure vanilla

Heat granulated sugar over medium-high heat, stirring constantly, until caramelized liquid forms. Remove from heat and add brown sugar, whisking until smooth. Gradually add heated cream until thoroughly incorporated and blend in vanilla. Serve with a scoop of praline ice cream on top and drizzle sauce over the entire dessert.

Makes $1^1/4$ cups

INGREDIENTS AND COOKING TERMS

Key Lime: One of the two varieties of lime available in this area of the world. They are the small limes and are more sour and stronger flavored than the larger Persian variety. Key limes grow in abundantly throughout Florida and the Caribbean, and they are essential to the traditional Floridian masterpiece, Key Lime Pie. When making key lime anything, try as hard as you can to find and use real key limes, and never use concentrates or extracts. The difference key limes make is not discernible only by picky eaters or gourmets. It is a very real and very substantial difference.

Masa Harina: dried, finely ground corn used in the preparation of tortillas. Can be effectively made by combining equal parts of corn meal and corn flour.

Old Bay Seasoning: a popular commercial seafood seasoning easily available in either the spice or seafood section of supermarket aisles nationwide.

Roux: Many of the recipes in this book call for roux, which is simply a thickener made by combining flour with some form of fat, typically butter, and carefully cooking until the flour loses its raw taste. Although white roux is most commonly used worldwide, Cajun and other Louisiana cooking often calls for brown roux. If you need a brown roux, heat some flour in a dry pan and stir constantly until it turns the color of cinnamon. Once browned, add some heated fat to form a paste.

Herbes de Provence: A blend of spices commonly used in the Mediterranean regions of France. It varies widely in quality and flavor depending on the manufacturer, but a fairly consistent version can be made by combining 1 tablespoon of dried thyme, chervil, tarragon, and marjoram, 1 teaspoon oregano, rosemary, and summer savory, $1/2$ teaspoon dried mint, and 2 finely crumbled Mediterranean bay leaves. This spice is very fragrant and every bit as magical as the Mediterranean itself. It's especially good on poultry and fish.

More tips on page 63.

Fried Flounder   Shrimp Salad   Thai Chicken   Mahi Mahi with Pecan, Butter, and Frangelico Sauce   Beer Boiled Shrimp

Flounder's Chowder and Ale House

Pensacola Beach, Florida

Flounder's Chowder and Ale House has, from small beginnings back in 1981, matured to become a top quality restaurant listed as one of *Florida Trend* Magazine's "Top 200 Restaurants." Flounder's now also frequently runs away with the annual "Best Seafood," "Best Place to Eat," "Best Bar with Live Entertainment," and other top honors by the *Pensacola News Journal.*

In addition to its reputation for the finest, freshest seafood in the Pensacola area and beyond, Flounder's has also made a name for itself in the entertainment field by featuring the best in reggae music in its unique beach bar during the summer season. With prized cuisine and the tropical rhythms of a reggae band, Flounder's is the place to be in Pensacola Beach.

Fortunately, Admiral Flounder has not forgotten the diverse history of the American people or the seafaring community. The restaurant flourishes with historical items from all over America, combined with objects d'art from its novel past. Flounder's also displays artifacts and other items from around the world that have made it to our shores in a number of fascinating ways. One of the most intriguing of such items is a refugee raft that made it here from Cuba after its occupants successfully escaped Castro's regime.

However, the main reason that Flounder's has undoubtedly established such a steadfast reputation as an exceptional restaurant can be attributed to Chef David Andrews (a.k.a. "Chef Crab"). Chef Andrews hails from New York and has been with Flounder's for 10 years. Our distinctive and award winning entrees acquire their special ambience thanks to Chef Andrews' expertise and his devotion to keeping Flounder's an exceptionally distinguished and celebrated restaurant.

Fried Flounder

Flounder filets (desired amount)

Egg wash
2 whole eggs
1 cup whole milk

Mix eggs and milk and beat well.

Breading
1 cup self rising flour
1 tablespoon Old Bay Seasoning or Prudholme
Seafood Seasoning
2 teaspoons black pepper
1 teaspoon salt
1 teaspoon granulated garlic
1 teaspoon paprika

Mix all ingredients together in a large mixing bowl.

Drench flounder filets heavily in egg wash and then in breading. Place in saucepan with oil preheated to 350 - 375 degrees. While cooking, make sure that flounder filets are completely covered. Cook until golden brown.

Yield is variable

Shrimp Salad

2^1/2 pounds (130-150 count)
  popcorn shrimp,
  peeled and cooked
1/8 teaspoon minced garlic
1/8 cup parsley flakes
1/2 cup red onion, chopped

1/2 cup celery, chopped
1/2 teaspoon salt
1/2 teaspoon black pepper
3/4 cup mayonnaise
Lettuce
Tomato wedges

Place precooked shrimp in a large mixing bowl. Add minced garlic and stir well. Add remaining ingredients, finishing with mayonnaise and mix well. Place over bed of lettuce. Add tomato wedges and cucumber slices for garnish.

Serves 4

Thai Chicken

1 cup brown sugar
1 cup Worcestershire sauce
1 cup pineapple juice
4 chicken breasts
Thai Sauce for Chicken (recipe below)

Mix together the brown sugar, Worcestershire sauce, and pineapple juice. Marinate the chicken in this mixture overnight. Grill marinated chicken on both sides until done.

Serves 4

Thai Sauce for Chicken

1 cup peanut butter
1 teaspoon sesame seeds
$1/2$ ounce sesame seed oil
1 teaspoon cayenne pepper

Mix all ingredients and store at room temperature. When needed, warm the sauce and pour generously over the chicken.

Serves 4

Mahi Mahi with Pecan, Butter, and Frangelico Sauce

1 tablespoon lemon
  pepper seasoning
1 tablespoon salt
1 tablespoon granulated garlic

2 cups melted butter
4 (8-ounce) portions mahi mahi filets
Pecan, Butter, and Frangelico Sauce
  (recipe on page 62)

Grilled Seasoned Mahi Mahi

Combine lemon pepper seasoning, salt, and granulated garlic. Set aside. Melt 2 cups of butter in a saucepan. Dip fish filets in butter, then sprinkle with the seasoning mixture. Grill filets until cooked to requirements, preferably over mesquite wood. Cover with Pecan, Butter, and Frangelico Sauce (next page).

Serves 4

Pecan, Butter, and Frangelico Sauce

$1/2$ cup pecan pieces
$1/2$ cup butter
$1/4$ cup light brown sugar
4 shots of Frangelico liqueur

Mix pecan pieces and brown sugar and set aside. Melt butter in a saucepan and add pecan and sugar mixture. Bring to a boil. Add Frangelico and stir. Serve over fish.

Serves 4

Beer Boiled Shrimp

2 bottles dark beer (McGuire's Ale)
$1/3$ cup liquid crab boil
1 teaspoon cayenne pepper
$1/4$ cup lemon juice
$1/2$ cup Old Bay Seasoning
2 teaspoons salt
2 fresh lemons, cut in halves
4 pounds (36-40) medium or large shrimp

Fill a large pot $3/4$ full with water and bring to a boil. Add all ingredients, except shrimp, and bring to a boil again. Add shrimp and cook for 5 minutes, stirring frequently until done. Strain and serve (shell optional) with cocktail sauce and fresh lemon wedges.

Serves 4-8

HINTS AND TIPS

FOR FISH

An average-size single serving of fish weighs approximately $1/2$ pound.

Save and freeze any fish bones and carcasses that you would ordinarily throw out. They provide the essential ingredients for a fish stock and can be used to enhance the flavor of any seafood chowder or bisque.

Lemons and limes (and just about any other citrus fruit) add a magic touch to fish. Serve fresh, sliced citrus as an accompaniment to fish. You can also use citrus juices to marinate fish; try submerging your fillets in lemon or lime juice for approximately $1/2$ hour. (Any longer, and the fish begins to "cook.")

You should remove fish from the refrigerator $1/2$ hour before you cook it.

You can tell when your fish is cooked by flaking it with a fork. If it flakes easily, it is done. Or, if the filet is very thick, check the middle. It is done when it loses its translucent quality.

To neutralize the odor of cooking fish, burn a little sugar in a pan covered with aluminum foil.

Fish is probably the most frustrating thing in the world to grill, so here is what you can do to make it a little easier for you. When you grill fish, make the grill very hot and make sure cooking surface is well oiled. Also brush the fish with oil. Continue to oil the fish from time to time. This is all you can do to prevent the fish from sticking on the bars and breaking up when you turn it over or try to remove it. When the outside of the fish is sealed, finish cooking it under moderate heat.

Using clarified butter when you saute fish will greatly improve its flavor.

*More tips on page 87.

Bacon Wrapped Tuna a la Fud   Chargrilled Chicken a la Fud
Squashed Crab Soup   Couch Potatoes

Fudpucker's Beachside Bar and Grill

Fort Walton Beach, Florida / Destin, Florida

If you're looking for a place that is "Famous For Food and Fun," then your very best bet is Fudpucker's Beachside Bar and Grill. Fudpucker's began in 1982 as a snack bar in a local nightclub. Back then the only things you could find on the menu were Fudburgers, Fishpuckers, Chickenpuckers, and French fries. From these rather inauspicious beginnings, Fudpucker's has grown into one of the must-see places on the Emerald Coast. Today, our two locations offer extensive menus featuring seafood, salads, burgers, chicken, and all manner of great food.

Fudpucker's has also become a destination for those who seek the very best in live entertainment. Our local talent is unparalleled and we offer everything from the great ballads of the sixties to the foot stomping sounds of Zydeco and Cajun music. And, Fudpucker's is a place where you can be yourself, let your hair down, kick back and enjoy the casual island (sorta nautical) atmosphere. In fact, if the urge strikes you to write on the walls, then feel free to do so. But we do ask that you do not use lipstick.

Chester Kroeger has been the man with the plan ever since founding Fudpucker's back in 1982. He began his cooking career at age four. After watching his parents cook lunch one day, he decided that he could do it too. He concocted a witch's brew that fateful day. Near its completion, Chester felt that his brew wasn't bubbling enough, and in his efforts to improve its state he added soap. Needless to say, it bubbled, and Chester proudly served his creation to the only person he could find -- a guest at his parents hotel. Chester recalls that the poor old woman took one taste before spitting it out and rocketing off in pursuit of the young chef. He managed to find safety behind his father while the lady ranted on about being poisoned. Unfortunately, he paid a high price for his amateur culinary endeavors over his father's knee. Not to be daunted, Chester continued his culinary pursuits by cooking for his family on a regular basis until he left for college. At the University of West Florida, Chester's dorm always smelled great with mouthwatering aromas permeating the air, regardless of the campus rule against cooking. His legendary parties became known as "Shrimp and Oyster Orgies," and he earned a reputation as a gourmet cook (not hard to do in college).

Chester started Fudpucker's a few years after graduating college with a degree in Public Administration and Coastal Zone Management -- not exactly the required course work for a restauranteur. He got into business because he loved the feel of it and he loved food. He still loves food, although maybe a little bit too much these days.

Chester's philosophy of cooking is that to be a great cook you can't be afraid to try anything. Yes, you will make mistakes. But that is how you learn.

Lately, Chester has been turning his attention toward Cuban and Caribbean cuisine. It is likely, he says, that these influences will soon be reflected in Fudpucker's menu.

Bacon Wrapped Tuna a la Fud

"Fresh tuna is an absolutely wonderful fish. It is more like a steak in that it's firm and very lean. Because it has so little fat it can dry out if not prepared properly. My suggestion is to serve it just like you would a steak -- medium or medium-rare. By doing so, you will keep the fish from drying out, thus truly enhancing the quality of its flavor. While you've got your grill on, why not complement your bacon wrapped tuna with some chargrilled veggies? Simply prepare some cross-cut red bell peppers, carrot sticks, onion rings, and sliced zucchini or yellow squash, coat them lightly with olive oil, place them on the grill, spice as you wish, and cook to your satisfaction. You might want to try some fettucine alfredo as a side to round out your meal. It's a great complement."

Several 8-ounce tuna portions
Thinly sliced bacon
1/2 cup soy sauce
1/4 cup Worcestershire sauce
4 tablespoons honey
Black Pepper, to taste

Wrap portions of fresh tuna with thinly sliced bacon using toothpicks to secure the bacon to the tuna. Place on the grill. Make a basting sauce by combining the soy sauce, Worcestershire, and honey and brush onto the tuna. Cook until the edges appear done or until tuna begins to lighten in color and bacon begins to sizzle. Turn. Be very careful when turning fish over as it may fall apart. Cook until done to your personal taste. Chester recommends medium-rare to medium. Brush once again with basting sauce. Dust tuna lightly with black pepper before serving.

Yield is variable

Chargrilled Chicken a la Fud

"I especially like this dish with chutney as a complement. I typically use Major Grey's Mango Chutney because it's easily available and tastes great. I also tend to serve this dish with rice -- preferably Spanish or yellow rice with some wild rice added for extra flavor and texture. Try some spicy jalapeno cornbread with this dish if you have time to prepare it. It's a great addition that adds a "homey" touch to the meal."

Several chicken breasts

$^1/_2$ cup soy sauce

$^1/_4$ cup Worcestershire sauce

4 tablespoons honey

Cooked bacon strips (2 per chicken breast)

Monterey Jack cheese, sliced

Black pepper, to taste

Select several chicken breasts and place onto grill. Make a basting sauce by combining the soy, Worcestershire, and honey. Brush chicken lightly with the basting sauce while cooking. Cook product until the edges appear done or the chicken begins to lighten in color. Turn over. Brush once again with basting sauce. Place 2 pieces of cooked bacon on top of the chicken and top with 2 slices of Monterey Jack Cheese. Cook until the cheese melts slightly. Dust product with black pepper before serving.

Yield is variable

Squashed Crab Soup

"I can't say enough about this soup. Suffice it to say that it is beyond awesome! I readily recommend it as a meal starter as well as a main course. You might wish to try it with "Wheatsworth" crackers -- somehow their "whole wheat goodness" adds an earthy quality to the soup."

Thickener for Soup

$1/2$ pint half and half
$1/2$ pint milk
$1/2$ cup flour

In a medium sized mixing bowl, combine flour and small portions of milk until a smooth paste is formed. Add the remainder of the milk and the half & half and mix thoroughly. Set aside.

Soup

$1/4$ pound butter
1 lb crab meat (claw or lump)
1 pound onions, chopped
2 pounds squash, thinly sliced
$1/4$ cup crab base (or shrimp base)
1 quart water

1 teaspoon garlic powder
1 teaspoon cayenne pepper
$1/2$ cup carrots, grated
$1/4$ cup chives, cut
2 teaspoons salt

Melt butter in a large stock pot. Add carrots, onions, and squash and cook until the squash begins to fall apart. Add garlic powder, cayenne pepper, salt, and crab base and mix thoroughly while simmering. Add the chives, crab meat, and water and bring to a boil. Add the thickener for soup in small quantities. Continue stirring until the soup thickens. Reduce heat and simmer for 10 minutes, stirring occasionally.

Couch Potatoes

"Great as appetizers, munchies, or as a starch with your main meal. Try serving them with a traditional sour cream or homemade ranch dressing. My favorite is the ranch because it adds a tanginess that blends well with the spices in the couch potatoes."

1 pint egg wash (eggs, milk, salt to taste)

4 pounds potatoes, baked and peeled

1/4 pound bacon, cooked and crumbled

3 cups onion, finely diced

2 tablespoon bacon drippings

1 teaspoon white pepper

1/4 teaspoon red pepper

1/4 cup chives

1/4 pound cooked broccoli, finely chopped

1/4 pound cheddar cheese, grated

1/2 cup sour cream

1 teaspoon blackening spice for fish

1 pint egg wash (2 eggs, 1 cup milk, and salt to taste)

2 cups breading mix (a mixture of bread crumbs, cracker meal, flour, salt, and pepper)

In a large mixing bowl, combine all ingredients except eggwash and breading mix. Blend thoroughly. Place in refrigerator and chill thoroughly. Scoop out 2-ounce portions and hand form into oblong shapes resembling potatoes. Dip into egg wash, coating thoroughly. Roll in breading mix until coated. Fry in 350 degree peanut oil until golden brown. Serve with your favorite accompaniment.

West Indies Salad　White Wine Garlic Butter　Frangelico Butter

Harbor Docks

Destin, Florida

Back in 1979, Harbor Docks was anchored in a weather-beaten little cottage on the docks of the Destin Harbor. At that time, it furnished only six picnic tables where the local crowd gathered for an evening feast of ice cold beer and oysters on the half shell while an ancient dog named Raspberry mellowed out on the porch thumping his tail at all the hungry folks.

Harbor Docks was nothing fancy in its early days, and, except for its size, things haven't changed much. The locals still find the atmosphere truly inviting and the food better than ever. Charles Morgan, the owner of Harbor Docks, has added on to the little cottage over the years; now the deck sprawls along the waterfront, making it one of the most spectacular restaurants on the Emerald Coast. As for the visitors, Harbor Docks has become the birthplace for many memorable nights of wonderful dining. You can treat yourself to dinner in the picture-flanked dining room or out on one of the many waterfront decks that provide cool harbor breezes even on the hottest of summer nights. Harbor Docks also has an authentic sushi bar for guests who prefer to try something a little more exotic.

Of course, Raspberry has gone on to his rewards, and Morgan has added other modern conveniences; he installed air conditioning about ten years ago, paved the parking lot, and added valet parking. But the picnic tables are still here, as is the "little cottage" atmosphere that has made so many guests over the years feel right at home. You can still find a lot of the old favorites on the menu, or you can try some of the more exotic specialties at the authentic sushi bar. Whatever you choose, you will find our food honest and healthy and our service warm, friendly, and helpful. Harbor Docks invites you to relax and enjoy the view and soak in the local color . . . the local flavor of Harbor Docks.

West Indies Salad

1 pound crab meat
1 small red onion, thinly sliced
1 teaspoon oregano
2 lemon squeezes
$1/2$ teaspoon garlic

$1/2$ teaspoon salt
$1/2$ teaspoon black pepper
2 ice cubes
1 cup zesty Italian salad dressing

Mix all ingredients together in a large bowl with a spoon. Chill and serve on a bed of lettuce. Garnish with tomatoes and lemons. Serve with crackers or garlic bread.

Serves 4

White Wine Garlic Butter

"Great for use on all grilled and broiled seafood"

1 bunch green onions, finely chopped
3 cloves garlic, finely chopped
1 bunch parsley, finely chopped
4 ounces capers
3 cups white wine Chablis
4 pounds butter solids

Add all ingredients to the wine. Cook on high heat until mixture reduces to approximately half. Add 4 pounds butter solids. Continue cooking for 4 minutes or until butter is melted.

Makes approximately 10 cups

Frangelico Butter

"Try using this sauce on breaded shrimp, fish, or chicken"

4 ounces clarified butter
2 ounces Frangelico liqueur
Salt, to taste
Pepper, to taste
Cayenne pepper, to taste
Granulated garlic, to taste

Heat butter and add about 2 ounces Frangelico liqueur. After the sauce flames up, cook until thoroughly heated. Season to taste. Pour butter over breaded items. Squeeze juice from one lemon wedge over the top for additional taste.

Makes 6 ounces

Handmade Southwestern Style Crab Tamales with Crushed Tomatoes,
Avocado and Habanero-Chipolte Creme Fraiche   Crab Cakes
Chocolate Chambord Pate   Butterscotch Almond Cheesecake

Hatteras Cafe

Destin, Florida

Hatteras Cafe, located on the second floor of the Destin Yacht Club, towers above the Emerald Coast with its five-star dining. Its superior quality and dedication to excellence have earned Hatteras Cafe a prestigious ranking in *Florida Trend* magazine's roster of the top 200 restaurants in Florida, making it one of the youngest restaurants ever to receive this coveted award. President and General Manager Frank Kovach immediately fell in love with Destin when he first sailed into port aboard his Hatteras Yacht. The Hatteras Yacht, regarded as one of the finest and most dependable boats ever made, provided an appropriate name for the restaurant Kovach was soon to begin.

Hatteras Cafe has become widely popular for its eclectic ethnic cuisine and is alive with "the taste of Destin." These dishes, created by Chef Andi Bell, start with only the finest, freshest ingredients and end as culinary masterpieces with innovative and ethnically vibrant undertones. The recipes in this section provide a small but tantalizing representation of the extraordinary cuisine that Chef Bell prepares.

Add to this unique and outstanding cuisine one of the most highly trained staffs in the world, and one is obliged to redefine the meaning of fine dining. For one hour prior to opening each evening, Hatteras Cafe's staff undergoes extensive instruction in the art of wine tasting, food preparation, and customer service, making the staff expertly capable of assisting customers in their food and drink selections. Such service is particularly helpful when it comes to selecting a wine from a menu of over eighty selections, twenty of which are available by the glass. Each guest is also greeted by the head waiter Bobby Marler, a third-generation Destin resident, who explains the pastry chef's creations and takes care of the customers during the evening to ensure that their visit is exceptional in every way. General manager Mark Finnerty, a ten-year restaurant veteran in Destin who has been aboard the Hatteras since its inception, guarantees an evening of "smooth sailing."

Hatteras Cafe's impeccable attention to customer satisfaction and detail have inspired the local clientele to establish two clubs in conjunction with the restaurant: The Hatteras Club (Hat Club) and the more exclusive Admiral's Club. Inquiries regarding membership may be directed to Sheila, Hatteras Cafe's friendly office manager.

When in Destin, you can experience this five-star food and service of the Hatteras Cafe with a panoramic view of the harbor as a spectacular backdrop. Hatteras Cafe prides itself on its elegance and its exquisite dining, and it ensures that every customer will experience a truly memorable evening.

Handmade Southwestern Style Crab Tamales with Crushed Tomatoes, Avocado, and Habanero-Chipolte Creme Fraiche

4 dried corn husks	**1 teaspoon salt**
2 cups masa harina	**1 teaspoon black pepper**
1 tablespoon chili powder	**1³/4 cups boiling water**
2 teaspoons cumin	**1 pound jumbo lump crab meat**
2 teaspoons coriander	**4 ounces hot sauce**

Soak corn husks in water for at least 8 hours. Fold masa and next 5 ingredients into boiling water. Spread mixture onto flattened, soaked corn husk. Divide crab meat among tamales, placing in center, then fold from side of corn husk and roll. Steam tamales in water and hot sauce for 10-15 minutes. Top with Habanero Creme Fraiche (recipe below) and serve hot with sliced avocado and chopped tomatoes.

Makes 4 tamales

Habanero Creme Fraiche

1 cup heavy whipping cream
1/4 cup buttermilk
1 tablespoon fresh habaneros, pureed

Combine heavy cream and buttermilk in a non-reactive container. Cover and let sit for 24 hours at room temperature. Add habanero puree and mix.

Makes 1¹/4 cups

Hatteras Cafe Crab Cakes

1 yellow sweet pepper, diced
1 red sweet pepper, diced
1 medium red onion, diced
2 whole eggs, beaten
$1/3$ cup heavy cream
3 pounds jumbo lump crab

4 cups bread crumbs
Salt, to taste
Pepper, to taste
Flour, for dusting
Olive oil
Lemon
Pecans

Sauté peppers and onion. Remove from heat and let cool. Mix beaten eggs, cream, crab, and bread crumbs. Salt and pepper to taste. Form mixture into equal portioned patties. Lightly dust with flour and sauté in olive oil until golden brown. Transfer to an oven proof dish and bake for 5 minutes. Serve with lemon and pecans.

Makes 16 cakes

Chocolate Chambord Pate

22 ounces dark Callebaut chocolate
1 pound unsalted butter
12 ounces chambord
8 egg whites, whipped to soft peaks

Melt chocolate, butter, and chambord over double boiler. Fold in whipped egg whites, half at a time. Pour into a plastic wrap lined loaf pan and chill over night. To serve, slice and place on a plate. Garnish with fresh mint.

Butterscotch Almond Cheesecake

Crust

1 cup flour
^{1}/3 cup sugar
^{1}/4 cup toasted almonds
^{1}/4 teaspoon salt
7 tablespoons chilled butter,
   cut into pieces
1 egg yolk
^{1}/4 teaspoon almond extract

Preheat oven to 350 degrees. Line a 9-inch spring form pan with foil. Butter and flour foil. Blend first 4 ingredients in processor until nuts are finely chopped. Add butter, yolk, and extract and blend until mixture coheres. Press onto bottom of spring form (not the sides). Bake until golden, about 20 minutes. Cool 10 minutes. Pull crust out of pan carefully. Remove foil and place crust back into pan.

Filling

4 (8-ounce) packages cream cheese (room temperature)
1^1/2 cups sugar
^{1}/4 cup scotch
1 tablespoon vanilla extract
4 eggs
2 cups sour cream

Beat cream cheese, 1^1/4 cups sugar, scotch, and vanilla in a large bowl until well blended. Add eggs, one at a time. Pour into crusted pan and bake until set (about 50 minutes). Place on rack and cool for 10 minutes. Mix sour cream with remaining ^{1}/4 cup of sugar. Spoon on top and bake for 10 more minutes.

Butterscotch topping

2 cups sugar
$2/3$ cup + 1 tablespoon scotch
$2/3$ cup whipping cream
$1/4$ cup butter
$3/4$ cup toasted almonds, coarsely
   chopped

Stir sugar and $2/3$ cup of scotch in a large sauce pan over medium heat until sugar dissolves. Increase heat and boil until syrup is a golden brown. Add cream and butter and stir until smooth. Cool 10 minutes. Stir in 1 tablespoon of scotch. Let stand until cool but still pourable, about 2 hours. Mix in almonds. Spoon topping over the cheesecake. Refrigerate 1 hour before releasing.

Makes 1 (9-inch) cake

Pistachio Encrusted Tuna with Tropical Fruit Beurre Blanc
Grilled Portobello Mushrooms with Crabmeat and Bernaise
Chilled Zucchini Soup   Honey Mustard   Lemon Ribbon Layered Meringue Pie

Jamie's French Restaurant

Pensacola, Florida

Few Emerald Coast restaurants so expertly and so completely capture the true 'spirit of the place' as Jamie's French Restaurant. Historically, Pensacola was an area marked by rivalries and claims of Old World powers, mainly by France and Spain. A French restaurant in an area known for its distinct Spanish colonial style, Jamie's is a meeting point for the myriad of colorful traditions that Pensacola embodies.

Drawing its atmosphere from Pensacola's historical Seville Square, Jamie's French Restaurant steps back in time to provide an elegant dining experience. For the past ten years, Jamie's has been serving fresh Gulf seafood, French classics such as foie gras and escargot, as well as wild game dishes -- all of them masterfully created by Elizabeth Dasher, a Culinary Institute of America graduate and creator of the special flavors that have distinguished Jamie's over the years. Although Chef Dasher is no longer with Jamie's, the tradition continues with Chef Michael Liebano, who now prepares the extraordinary cuisine for which Jaime's is famous.

Proprietor Gary Serafin acquired Jamie's because he wanted to share his love of fine food and wine with Pensacola. The results have been so consistently outstanding that for the past ten years Jamie's has been awarded a place in *Florida Trend* magazine's list of the Top 200 restaurants in Florida, and the *Wine Spectator's* "Award of Excellence" from 1992-1994. Jamie's commitment to serving award-winning cuisine ensures that customers will have an unparalleled experience in fine dining. With its private dining rooms, fine linen, and fireplaces, Jamie's enfolds its guests in an aura of elegance and comfort, making it an ideal choice for that special occasion or business dinner.

Pistachio Encrusted Tuna
with Tropical Fruit Beurre Blanc

1 egg	1/2 teaspoon powdered onion
1 1/2 cups milk	1/2 teaspoon salt
1 cup Pistachios	1/2 teaspoon black pepper
1 cup bread crumbs	1 cup flour
1 teaspoon curry powder	4 (6-ounce) tuna steaks
1/2 teaspoon powdered garlic	2 tablespoons olive oil

Combine egg and milk to make an egg wash. In a food processor, combine nuts, bread crumbs, and seasonings. Set up a breading station with three separate bowls: flour, egg wash, and nut mixture. Dredge tuna in flour, then in egg wash, then in nut mixture. Sauté tuna in 2 tablespoons olive oil over high heat until brown on both sides. Cook through in a 350 degree oven for approximately 5 minutes.

Tropical Fruit Beurre Blanc Sauce

3 tablespoons chopped shallots
1/2 cup white wine
1/2 pound butter, room temperature and cut into small pieces
1/2 cup mango, diced
1/4 cup kiwi, diced
1/4 cup pineapple, crushed
2 tablespoons key lime juice

In a flat bottom sauce pan, reduce shallots and wine until almost dry. Remove from heat and swirl in butter until a sauce forms. Fold fruit and key lime juice into sauce and spoon over tuna.

Serves 4

Grilled Portobello Mushrooms with Crab Meat and Bernaise

Marinade

- 1/4 cup Dijon mustard
- 1/4 teaspoon garlic, minced
- 1/4 teaspoon shallots, minced
- 1/4 cup Balsamic vinegar
- 1 cup olive oil

Combine all ingredients. Use this marinade for the mushrooms.

- 4 large Portobello mushrooms, stemmed
- 1/2 pound crab meat
- 1 tablespoon chopped scallion
- Salt, to taste
- Pepper, to taste

Place mushrooms in marinade for one hour. Grill over an open flame for approximately 2 minutes on each side. Heat crab, scallions, salt, and pepper in saute' pan.

Mound 1/4 of crab meat in center of plate. Slice each mushroom into five pieces and arrange around crab meat. Top with Bernaise-Hollandaise mixture (pg. 84) and serve.

Bernaise Sauce

1 tablespoon shallots, chopped
$1/2$ cup tarragon, dried
$1/4$ cup white wine
$1/4$ cup tarragon vinegar

Mix ingredients in a small sauce pot and reduce until all the liquid is gone. Cool and reserve.

Hollandaise Sauce

1 egg yolk
1 tablespoon white wine
1 tablespoon lemon juice
1 dash Tabasco
1 dash Worcestershire
$1/2$ pound butter melted and kept

Mix the egg, wine, lemon juice, Tabasco, and Worcestershire sauce together and heat in a stainless steel bowl over a pot of boiling water. Cook until the eggs thicken, stirring constantly. Do not overcook. Remove from heat. Add butter in a slow, steady stream. Fold the tarragon Bernaise mixture into Hollandaise.

Serves 4

Chilled Zucchini Soup

1/4 cup olive oil
1 medium onion, coarsely
   chopped (about 1 cup)
6-8 medium zucchini, scrubbed,
   trimmed, and cut into
   1/4-inch slices

2 cloves garlic minced
3 1/3 to 4 cups heavy cream
Pinch of thyme
Salt, to taste
Freshly ground black pepper,
   to taste

Heat oil in large heavy skillet over medium heat until rippling. Add onion. Sauté, stirring occasionally, until softened. Add zucchini and garlic. Reduce heat to low. Simmer covered until browned. Remove from heat. Stir in 2 cups of the heavy cream and the thyme. Let cool slightly.

Place half the zucchini mixture in blender or food processor. Blend until smooth. Transfer mixture to a large bowl. Stir in 1/3 cup of the heavy cream. Repeat procedure with remaining 1 cup heavy cream. Force mixture through a sieve.* Season with salt and pepper to taste. Refrigerate several hours before serving.

* If coarser texture is desired, do not put mixture through sieve.

Makes approximately 2 quarts

Honey Mustard

1 1/2 cups honey
1 1/2 cups mustard
1 cup lemon juice
3 cups salad oil
2 tablespoons curry

2 tablespoons dried mustard
2 tablespoons celery seed
2 tablespoons parsley
2 tablespoons chopped scallions

Pour all ingredients into a large mixing bowl and blend.

Lemon Ribbon Layered Meringue Pie

Crust

      1^1/2 cups chopped pecans
      2 tablespoons sugar
      2 tablespoons butter, softened

  Mix ingredients together and press firmly into a 9-inch pie pan. Bake in 400 degree oven for ten minutes or until crust is browned.

Lemon Curd

      6 tablespoons butter
      Zest of one lemon
      ^{1}/3 cup lemon juice
      ^{1}/8 teaspoon salt
      1 cup sugar
      2 whole eggs
      2 egg yolks

  Melt butter. Add lemon zest, lemon juice, salt, and sugar. Slightly beat eggs with yolks. Combine with other mixture until and cook over boiling water, beating constantly with a whisk until thick and smooth.

  In the crust, layer 2 cups of vanilla ice cream, then half the curd and repeat. Top with meringue and brown.

Meringue

      3 egg whites
      ^{1}/3 cup sugar

  Combine ingredients and whip.

Makes 1 pie

HINTS AND TIPS

<u>FOR FISH</u>

Before sliding the fish into a pan of hot oil, pat the outside of the fish dry. Otherwise you, too, will be partially sauteed.

Before frying, make sure the surface of your fish is thoroughly dry before you dip it into flour, bread crumbs, or batter. This simple step will make your fried fish very crisp.

If you are going to dip the fish in an egg wash before frying, add a little sherry to the egg. It will give the fried fish an outstanding flavor.

Deep fried fish is done when it rises to the surface of the oil.

Since vegetable oils and fats absorb very little fish odor, you can strain and reuse them for frying fish in the future.

The best way to marinate something is in a plastic bag. Put the meat or vegetables and marinade in a bag, release all the air, and seal it tightly. This will keep your food thoroughly coated with the marinade without constantly flipping and rotating it.

Flounder is sometimes called sole in fishmarkets. Although flounder does resemble sole in taste and texture, it is more tender. Because of their similarities, sole and flounder can be interchanged in cooking.

When buying flounder, you may find that there are two different colors of flounder fillets. This is because the underside of a flounder is white meat while the top side is slightly grey. However, there is no difference in taste or texture between them.

A finely mashed anchovy or two imparts a delicious accent to any fish, chicken, or meat sauce.

More tips on page 113.

Rigatoni with Roasted Chicken and Sweet Peppers   Roasted Chicken with Garlic and Vegetables   Marinated, Grilled Fajita Steak with Corn Relish   Grilled Venison Sausage with Caramelized Onions   Louisiana Crab Cakes with Sauce Piquante   Crispy Fried Calamari with Remoulade Sauce   Caesar Salad   Maytag Bleu Cheese Dressing   Vegetable Stock   Roasted Sweet Pepper Soup   Seafood Bisque   Corleone   Chocolate Sin Cake with Espresso Cream   Chocolate Sauce   Mango Sauce   Rasberry Coulis   Pecan Pie   Key Lime Cheesecake

Marina Cafe

Destin, Florida

The cuisine at Marina Cafe exemplifies a cuisine developed totally from the love of great food prepared in a classical style with regional influences, or the combinations of various cuisines with the freshest products found locally or imported from overseas. Chef Tim Creehan creates dishes inspired by his customers' love of exciting, trend setting dishes and carefully prepared classical favorites. Thanks to Chef Creehan's South Louisiana background, many of the dishes at Marina Cafe have their roots deep in Louisiana tradition -- tradition that was developed and refined by generations of mothers, fathers, grandparents, and friends throughout the state. Chef Creehan explains that "starting as an apprentice to this intimidating world of cuisines, I was fortunate to have been raised in the location of the only true American cuisine, and at that time, the craze of the food world." Like all of the dishes at Marina Cafe, the Cajun and Creole wonders are prepared with honesty and authenticity as the standards of excellence.

Chef Tim Creehan's accolades include various awards in competition sanctioned by the American Culinary Federation. These awards include a 2nd place finish in the 1989 Florida Governor's Cup Seafood Challenge; 1st place in the 1987 Seafood Challenge of Baton Rouge; 2nd place in the 1987 Seafood Challenge of Louisiana; 4 awards in 7 categories at the 1987 Acadiana Culinary Classic (2 golds, a silver, and a bronze); and 4 medals in the 1987 Baton Rouge Culinary Classic. Other achievements include the best of show award in the 1992 annual Emerald Coast Chef's Challenge, including a 1st place finish in the dessert and signature series entree categories. Tim Creehan has been selected as a member of the Great Chefs of America since 1989. At age 26, Chef Creehan has become not only one of the youngest Certified Executive Chefs in America, but also one of the most accomplished. These awards are hallmarks of a chef who prepares dishes with unmatched quality, distinction, and expertise. With all of Chef Creehan's achievements, it is hardly surprising that *Florida Trend* magazine continually places Marina Cafe in its list of Florida's top 200 restaurants.

At Marina Cafe, one can dine casually and experience new American cuisines creatively prepared and artistically presented, or enjoy an elegant pairing of fine wine with traditionally prepared classics. The backdrop to this elegance is the Destin Harbor, frequently painted amber and gold from westerly sunsets. The tasteful possibilities are only limited to the diner's imagination. The food selected and prepared by the restaurant's dedicated staff represents the enthusiasm of young American chefs and their will to challenge the palate and the expectations of a seasoned proprietor, Jim Altamura.

Rigatoni with Roasted Chicken and Sweet Peppers

$^1/2$ pound rigatoni,
   cooked and chilled
1 chicken, roasted
$^3/4$ cup olive oil
$^1/2$ red sweet pepper, julienned

$^1/2$ gold sweet pepper, julienned
3 tablespoons basil, chopped
1 tablespoon garlic, chopped
Salt, to taste
Crushed red pepper, to taste
Romano cheese, grated

Remove the skin from the chicken and debone the meat. Cut the meat into julienne strips. Heat the olive oil in a large sauté pan. Add the peppers, basil, garlic, chicken, salt and red pepper. Sauté for 2 minutes. Add the pasta and toss until the pasta is heated thoroughly. Serve with grated Romano cheese.

Serves 4

Roasted Chicken with Garlic and Vegetables

2 whole chickens, split
Salt, to taste
Granulated garlic, to taste
Cayenne pepper, to taste
2 tablespoons rosemary, chopped
10 cloves garlic
1 tablespoon lemon juice

2 carrots, cut into 1-inch
   segments
2 baking potatoes, diced large
$^1/2$ cup olive oil
$^1/2$ cup parsley, chopped
2 cups water
$^1/2$ cup white wine

Preheat an oven to 425 degrees. Season the chickens to taste with salt, garlic and cayenne pepper. Place the chickens in a roasting pan with all of the remaining ingredients except the parsley. Roast the chickens for 30 minutes or until brown and crisp and clear runs from a pricked thigh. Serve the chickens with the roasted vegetables, reduced sauce, and garnish with chopped parsley.

Serves 4

Marinated, Grilled Fajita Steak with Corn Relish

Flank Steak

1 (2-pound) flank steak
$^1/_2$ cup canola oil
$^1/_4$ cup soy sauce
2 tablespoons lime juice

1 tablespoon garlic, chopped
1 tablespoon black pepper
1 cup sour cream

Marinate the flank steak in the canola oil, soy sauce, lime juice, garlic and black pepper for at least 1 hour, turning periodically. Preheat a grill surface.

Corn Relish

1 can of corn
1 red onion, diced
1 tomato, diced
1 jalapeno, diced

$^1/_2$ bunch cilantro, chopped
2 tablespoons honey
Salt, to taste

Prepare the relish by combining all of the ingredients in a mixing bowl and season to taste with salt. Let stand 30 minutes.

Grill the fajita steak to desired doneness and slice thinly across the grain. Serve garnished with the sour cream and prepared relish.

Serves 4

Grilled Venison Sausage with Caramelized Onions

4 pounds boneless pork meat
5 pounds boneless venison meat
10 large yellow onions
3 bunches green onions
1 cup garlic clove
1/2 cup thyme

Salt, to taste
Black pepper, to taste
Cayenne pepper, to taste
1/2 stick butter
1 tablespoon sugar

Cube the pork and venison into 1-inch pieces. Peel 5 of the onions and coarsely chop. Remove the green onion bottoms and coarsely chop. Run all of the ingredients through a meat grinder with a medium to large grinding plate. Begin with the meat products and finish with the vegetables and herbs, followed by a small piece of bread to clear the remaining ingredients from the grinder.

In a mixing bowl, blend all of the ingredients thoroughly and season to taste with salt, black pepper and cayenne pepper by cooking small patties to adjust seasonings.

Form into 4-ounce patties or stuff into sausage casings.

To make caramelized onions, julienne the 5 remaining onions. Melt the butter in a sauté pan. Add onions and sugar and cook until brown, stirring continuously. Season to taste with salt and black pepper.

Preheat a grill surface. Grill the sausage links or patties and serve with the caramelized onions and your favorite sweet mustard.

This recipe makes approximately 10 pounds of sausage which freezes well.

Serves 10

Louisiana Crab Cakes with Sauce Piquante

Louisiana Crab Cakes

1 pound jumbo lump crab meat
3 eggs
2 green onions, chopped
2 teaspoons garlic, chopped
1 tablespoon lemon juice
2 tablespoons sherry

2 teaspoons curry powder
$1/4$ cup Romano cheese, grated
4 cups bread crumbs
Salt, to taste
Cayenne pepper, to taste

Blend all of the crab cake ingredients in a mixing bowl. Mix together carefully avoiding breaking the crab meat lumps. Form into 2 x 2 inch square cakes $1/4$-inch thick.

Sauté or grill the cakes until heated throughout and serve with the prepared Sauce Piquante.

Sauce Piquante

$1/4$ cup onion, chopped
$1/4$ cup celery, chopped
$1/4$ cup bell pepper, chopped
$1/2$ jalapeno, chopped
2 cloves garlic, chopped

1 tablespoon butter
$1/2$ cup chicken stock
1 cup tomato puree
$1/4$ cup green onion, chopped
Salt, to taste

Sauté the onions, celery, bell pepper, jalapeno, and garlic in the butter for 5 minutes. Add the chicken stock, tomato puree, and green onion and bring to a slow boil for 15 minutes. Season to taste with salt and keep hot.

Serves 8

Crispy Fried Calamari with Remoulade Sauce

Fried Calamari

1 pound baby squid, cleaned
2 cups white flour
2 tablespoons black pepper

1 teaspoon cayenne pepper
1 teaspoon granulated garlic
1 tablespoon salt

Preheat a deep fryer to 375 degrees. Cut the cleaned squid in $3/4$ inch segments and toss in the flour seasoned with salt, granulated garlic, black pepper, and cayenne pepper, shaking off all the excess flour.

Deep fry the calamari for 3 to 5 minutes. Serve immediately with the prepared Remoulade Sauce.

Remoulade Sauce

1 cup mayonnaise
$1/4$ cup Creole mustard
2 tablespoons horseradish
1 tablespoon red wine vinegar

Blend all of the ingredients thoroughly in a mixing bowl.

Serves 6

Caesar Salad

2 cups French bread, cubed
$1/4$ cup butter, melted
2 egg yolks
1 tablespoon Dijon mustard
1 tablespoon garlic, chopped
1 teaspoon anchovy, ground
1 teaspoon lemon juice

1 tablespoon Worcestershire sauce
$1/4$ cup red wine vinegar
$3/4$ cup olive oil
Black pepper, to taste
1 head romaine lettuce
1 cup Romano cheese, grated

Toss the diced French bread with the melted butter and brown in a 400 degree oven for 5 minutes or until brown and crisp.

In a mixing bowl, blend the eggs, mustard, garlic, anchovies, lemon juice, Worcestershire sauce, and vinegar with a wire whip. Mixing continuously, slowly add the olive oil and season to taste with black pepper.

Cut and wash the romaine lettuce in ice water. Toss the lettuce with the dressing, croutons, and grated Romano cheese.

Serves 4

Maytag Bleu Cheese Dressing

1 pound Maytag bleu cheese, crumbled
3 cups olive oil
2 tablespoons garlic, chopped

$1/4$ cup basil, chopped
1 cup red wine vinegar
Salt, to taste
Black pepper, to taste

Blend all of the ingredients in a mixing bowl and chill. Serve over your favorite selection of mixed greens.

Vegetable Stock

"There are situations with particular food preparations when the products necessary to produce a meat, poultry, or seafood stock are not readily available. A simple vegetable stock is a good substitute in this situation. Whenever a recipe calls for a certain stock and it is not available, a vegetable stock is certainly more flavorful than water."

1/2 cup olive oil
4 large yellow onions
4 ribs celery
3 large carrots
2 heads garlic
3 tomatoes (canned whole or fresh)

2 sprigs parsley
2 tablespoons whole thyme
2 bay leaves
1 tablespoon black peppercorn
2 cups white wine

Heat the olive oil in a 4 to 5 gallon stock pot and sauté the vegetables and spices until the vegetables are lightly brown. Flambe with white wine and fill the stock pot 4 inches from the top with warm water.

Bring the stock to a rapid boil for 1 hour and remove from the heat. Strain through a fine sieve or chinois and allow to cool.

Roasted Sweet Pepper Soup

"Requested by Gourmet magazine"

15 red or gold sweet peppers
1 quart chicken stock
1 tablespoon garlic, chopped
3 tablespoons tomato paste

Salt, to taste
Crushed red pepper, to taste
3 tablespoons olive oil
12 large basil leaves, chopped

Roast the sweet peppers over an open flame until the skins are completely charred. Place the peppers in a brown paper bag and allow to cool for 15 minutes.

Remove the sweet peppers from the bag and rinse the charred skins off under cool running water. Remove the stems and seeds from the peppers and puree in a food processor or blender.

Heat the chicken stock in a heavy bottom pot and add the pureed peppers, garlic, and tomato paste. Bring to a slow boil for 25 minutes.

Season to taste with salt and crushed red pepper. Finish with olive oil and basil shortly before serving.

Seafood Bisque

1 stick butter
1/2 onion, diced
1 tablespoon garlic, chopped
1/2 rib celery, diced
1 cup Italian plum tomatoes, crushed
1/2 cup white flour
1/4 cup sherry
1 cup white wine
2 cups heavy cream
1 quart milk
2 ounces scallops
4 ounces baby shrimp
2 ounces crawfish tails
2 ounces crab meat
1 cup clams (with juice)
10 ounces fish, diced
1 teaspoon lemon juice
1/2 bunch green onion, chopped
1 teaspoon paprika
2 tablespoons basil, chopped
Salt, to taste
Black pepper, to taste
Cayenne pepper, to taste

Melt the butter in a heavy bottom pot and sauté the onions, garlic, celery, and tomatoes for 10 minutes. Stir in the flour until all is incorporated. Slowly add sherry, white wine, cream and milk, stirring continuously. Bring to a slow boil. Add all of the seafood ingredients, lemon juice, green onions and paprika. Bring back to a slow boil. Simmer for 20 to 30 minutes. Add the basil and season to taste with salt, black pepper and cayenne pepper.

Serves 12

Corleone

"Requested by Gourmet Magazine"

1 cup almonds, sliced and blanched
1/4 cup pecans, shelled
1/2 cup white chocolate, chopped
1/2 cup dark chocolate, chopped
1 tablespoon cinnamon
2 teaspoons nutmeg
3/4 cup graham cracker crumbs
2 cups honey
12 scoops vanilla ice cream

Blend all of the ingredients except the honey, ice cream, and mint in a food processor. Chop until a fine texture is achieved.

Roll each scoop of vanilla ice cream in the Corleone mixture until completely coated. Serve the Corleones in wine glasses topped with honey and garnished with fresh mint.

Serves 12

Chocolate Sin Cake with Espresso Cream

15 ounces semisweet chocolate
15 ounces unsalted butter
12 large eggs
2 cups sugar
1/2 portion Raspberry Coulis
   (recipe in this section)
1 mint leaf

Espresso Cream
   (recipe in this section)
Chocolate Sauce
   (recipe in this section)
Mango Sauce
   (recipe in this section)
Rasberry Coulis (recipe this section)

Preheat oven to 350 degrees. Butter the bottom of a 10-inch round cake pan and line the bottom with wax paper. Combine the chocolate and butter. Melt the butter and chocolate completely over a double boiler and let cool.

Whip the eggs and sugar together until foamy. Combine the 2 mixtures together and blend thoroughly. Pour the sin cake mixture into the cake pan and place the cake pan in a baking pan with at least 1 1/2 inches of water.

Bake for 45 minutes. Turn off the oven and allow the cake to cool in the oven. Refrigerate the cake for 2 hours before removing from the pan.

Espresso Cream

3 cups heavy cream
1 cup sugar
2 tablespoons espresso, ground

Blend the heavy cream and sugar in a mixing bowl and whip until stiff peaks form. Fold in the espresso grounds.

Chocolate Sauce

4 ounces semisweet chocolate
3/4 cup heavy cream

Combine the chocolate and cream in a mixing bowl and melt over a double boiler stirring continuously. Allow to cool to room temperature.

Mango Sauce

2 mangos, peeled and seeded
1/4 cup sugar
2 tablespoons heavy cream

Puree the mangos, sugar and cream in a food processor until smooth. Chill.

Raspberry Coulis

2 pints raspberry
1 cup powdered sugar
1/2 cup water

Puree all of the ingredients in a blender. Over a medium fire, bring the coulis to a slow boil for 10 minutes. Remove from the heat and pass through a very fine sieve or chinois. Add additional water if the coulis is too thick. Chill.

Place the 3 sauces in squeeze bottles. Decorate the base of 12 dessert plates. Slice the sin cake into 12 equal slices and place in the center of the plates. Place the espresso cream in a pastry bag with a star tip. Pipe the cream on the top of each slice and garnish with fresh mint.

Serves 12

Pecan Pie

Crust

4 cups white flour
2 eggs
2 egg yolks

1 pound butter, chipped
$^1/_3$ teaspoon salt
$^2/_3$ cup sugar

Blend all of the ingredients together. Mix by hand until all of the butter is incorporated and the dough is smooth. Roll the dough until the desired thickness is achieved. Roll the dough onto the rolling pin and unroll over a 12-inch tart pan. Press the dough into the tart pan and cut the excess dough off the edges.

Preheat an oven to 375 degrees.

Filling

1 stick butter, melted
1 cup light corn syrup
1 cup sugar
3 large eggs, beaten

1 teaspoon vanilla
1 teaspoon lemon juice
1 pinch salt
$1^1/_4$ cups pecan, chopped

Blend all of the ingredients in a mixing bowl. Pour the mixture into the chilled pie shell (recipe below). Transfer the pie to the oven and bake for 25 minutes. Remove the pie from the oven and let stand 15 minutes before slicing to serve.

Serves 8

Key Lime Cheesecake

Crust

3/4 cup graham cracker crumbs
1/4 cup sugar
1/3 cup butter, melted

Preheat an oven to 325 degrees. Blend all of the ingredients together in a mixing bowl. Press into the bottom of a 10 x 3-inch springform pan. Place the crust in the oven and bake until the edges are brown. Remove from the oven and allow to cool.

Filling

2 pounds cream cheese
6 eggs
1 cup butter, melted
2 cups sugar

2 tablespoons vanilla
1 ounce white creme de cacao
1/4 cup key lime juice

Soften the cream cheese. Place all of the ingredients in a mixer with a wire whip attachment. Whip on medium speed until the batter is smooth and there are no cream cheese lumps. Pour this mixture into the springform pan. Place the cake in the oven and cook for 20 minutes. Reduce the temperature to 250 degrees. Cook for 30 minutes or until the center is firm to the touch. Turn the oven off and allow the cake to cool in the oven with the door closed for 20 minutes.

Serves 12

Steak and Mushroom Pie   Irish Stew
Corned Beef and Cabbage with Horseradish Sauce   Senate Bean Soup
Bread Pudding with Irish Whiskey Sauce

McGuire's Irish Pub and Brewery

Pensacola, Florida

One drive by McGuire's and you'll get the feeling that something special is happening here. Festive and fun, McGuire's Irish Pub is a throwback to grand old turn-of-the-century saloons, Irish and otherwise. Winner of *Florida Trend* magazine's Golden Spoon Award listing it as one of Florida's top restaurants, McGuire's offers a winning combination: fun with food, a sense of place, and top quality fare at great value-for-the-money prices. The Pub also represents a rekindling of the American love affair with beef, serving the best burgers in North Florida and peerless U.S.D.A. Certified Prime Steaks. But not only does McGuire's Irish Pub serve up some of the best food in Florida, it also has a remarkable atmosphere, full of good ole' Irish banter. Located in Pensacola's original old firehouse, McGuire's has the best true Irish entertainment south of Boston, and over 98,000 dollar bills signed by Irishmen of all nationalities cover the ceiling. And, to add to all this food and fun, McGuire's brews fine ales, porters, and stouts right on the premises. (Indeed, many cars in the Pensacola area and beyond proudly display green bumper stickers in praise of McGuire's brews!) McGuire's deserves a loud cheer for embellishing Pensacola with its merry presence, its outstanding cuisine, and its good spirits.

The owners, Molly and McGuire Martin, have created a loyal following since 1977 by serving the finest products available at the best possible price. They pledge to provide warm and friendly service to each of their guests by professional, sincere employees who truly give a damn! The staff at McGuire's has high standards of excellence and if they are not proud of it, they won't serve it!

Steak and Mushroom Pie

"On our menu, trimmin's from our filet mignon baked with fresh mushrooms in a sherry wine sauce and topped with a homemade pastry crust. Served with honey dipped carrots -- a delicious Irish meal with McGuire's highest recommendation."

$^1/_3$ cup butter or margarine
2 pounds beef tenderloin,
   cut in cubes
Salt, to taste
Pepper, to taste

Granulated garlic, to taste
2 medium onions, chopped
3 cups fresh mushrooms, sliced
3 cups Brown Gravy (recipe below)
$^1/_2$ cup Burgundy or other dry
   red wine

Melt butter in a Dutch oven or roasting pan. Add tenderloin pieces and cook until brown; do not overcook. Sprinkle with salt, pepper, and granulated garlic. Add onions and cook, stirring occasionally until they are transparent and tender. Remove from heat. Pour cooking juices into a saucepan for the gravy.

Return beef and onion mixture to low heat. Add mushrooms, brown gravy, and wine. Simmer until beef is tender. Spoon into a casserole or individual oven-proof dishes. Cover with puff pastry and seal to the edges of the casserole. Prick pastry with a fork or carve in a decorative design with the tip of a knife. Bake at 375 degrees for 8 to 10 minutes or until the pastry is puffed and brown.

Brown Gravy

$^1/_2$ cup flour
2-3 cups beef bouillon or stock
Salt, to taste
Pepper, to taste

Over low heat, slowly add flour to juices from beef to make a roux. Stir in bouillon or stock as needed to make 3 cups of gravy. Add salt and pepper to taste.

Serves 4

Irish Stew

"No, this is not McGuire's daughter Amy, a stew on Continental's Newark to Paris flight. But like Amy, this is very spicy."

Oil
3 pounds of inside round,
  cut into 1 inch cubes
2 cups beef broth or stock
1 tablespoon granulated garlic
1 tablespoon salt
1 tablespoon pepper
18 small new potatoes, whole,
  with skin

4 ribs celery, cut into 1-inch pieces
2 medium onions,
  cut in half then quartered
2 cups frozen green beans
2 cups sliced fresh mushrooms
1 cup frozen green peas, thawed
4 large carrots, cut into 1 inch pieces

Heat a small amount of oil in a roasting pan or Dutch oven. Add beef and cook until just brown. Add broth, garlic, salt, and pepper, and simmer over low heat until beef is tender.

In a separate pot, cover potatoes with water and cook until tender. Add carrots, celery, and onion to beef and cook until almost done. Add potatoes and green beans and heat until the beans are hot. (If needed, thicken juices with a browned roux.) Add mushrooms. Spoon into bowls and garnish with peas.

Serves 6

Senate Bean Soup

"Same recipe as served in the U.S. Senate for 18 cents. (Can you believe these are the same guys who spend $237.00 for an 18-cent aircraft bolt? If they can do it, so can we!")

1¹/₂ pounds (one bag) dried navy beans
2 large onions
3 stalks celery
1 clove garlic
2 carrots

1 cup ham, diced
6 sprigs fresh parsley
1 teaspoon thyme
Salt, to taste
Pepper, to taste

Rinse beans in cold water. Check carefully for rocks and pebbles and cover with water. Soak at least 8 hours or overnight. Drain and return beans to the pot. Cover with 5 inches of water.

Finely chop onions, celery, garlic, and carrots and add to pot. Add the ham and the remaining ingredients. Bring to a boil, reduce heat, and simmer until beans are tender. (Caution: Watch this carefully and add water as needed or it will burn. Keep beans covered with water at all times and stir often.) Season to taste. This is really best prepared a day ahead of time and reheated. The soup thickens and the flavors develop. Serve hot with a bottle of Tabasco and a bottle of McGuire's Irish Ale.

Serves 8-10

Corned Beef and Cabbage with Horseradish Sauce

"On the menu, an Emerald Isle serving of corned beef with horseradish sauce, cabbage, Kilarney potatoes, and corn on the cob."

2 heads green cabbage
2 slices bacon
1 quart water
1 chicken bouillon cube

1 teaspoon salt
1 pound corned beef round,
   thinly sliced*

* We use Hebrew National brand, probably hard to find outside of New York City or Miami.

Wash cabbage, removing tough outer leaves. Cut in half. Remove most of the core. (Do not completely core the cabbage or it will fall apart and be difficult to handle.)

In a large pot, cook the bacon until almost crisp. Add water, chicken base, and salt. Boil 15 to 20 minutes. Add cabbage halves and cook until tender. Place the corned beef in a colander or steamer pan over the cabbage and heat through. While the cabbage is cooking, prepare the horseradish sauce. When the corned beef is done, remove it from water immediately to prevent overcooking. Do not rinse.

Horseradish Sauce

1 tablespoon butter or margarine
1 tablespoon flour
2 cups milk
2 tablespoons prepared horseradish
Salt and pepper, to taste

Over low heat, melt the butter and slowly stir in the flour to make a roux. Do not brown. Slowly add milk. Cook, stirring constantly, over medium heat until thick and creamy. Add horseradish and remove from heat. Cover to keep warm. Season to taste.

To serve, place one piece of cabbage on a plate. Top with 1/4 of the corned beef. Cover with sauce or serve on the side.

Serves 4

Bread Pudding with Irish Whiskey Sauce

"Homemade daily at McGuire's from an old Irish recipe. The sauce especially makes this a great combination."

Pudding

1/2 pound dried mixed fruit	1 tablespoon pure vanilla extract
2 teaspoons flour	1 loaf day-old French bread, cubed
4 cups whole milk	1/2 cup raisins
7 eggs	1 teaspoon nutmeg
2 cups granulated sugar	

Toss dried fruit with flour and finely chop. Set aside.

Scald milk over low heat -- do not boil. Whip eggs until frothy; slowly stir in sugar and whip until smooth. Add sugar and egg mixture to scalded milk. Stir in vanilla.

Place bread cubes in a deep 13x9-inch baking dish. Sprinkle with fruit and raisins. Pour milk and egg mixture over bread. Using the back of a large spoon or ladle; press the bread down into the pan so that the milk mixture is absorbed. Sprinkle with nutmeg. Place pan into a larger pan filled with 1 inch of water. Bake at 350 degrees for 45 minutes or until the top is a deep, golden brown.

Irish Whiskey Sauce

1/2 pound butter *	2 cups granulated sugar
4 eggs	1/3 cup Irish whiskey **

* *Margarine can be substituted, but with nearly a dozen eggs, what's a little butter?*
** *You could use any ol' American whiskey, but then again you could buy a frozen dessert at the grocery store . . .*

Melt butter over medium heat. Whip eggs until light and frothy. Slowly add sugar, beating continuously. Add melted butter and continue to beat over medium heat. When sugar is completely dissolved, remove from heat and stir in Irish whiskey.

This can be served warm straight from the oven or made ahead and reheated in a microwave prior to serving. Spoon a generous serving into a bowl and top with warm Whiskey sauce. ENJOY!

Destin Triggerfish with Lump Crab and Caper Meuniere   Stuffed Roasted
Peppers   Vine Ripened Tomato Le Caprese Salad with Mozzarella
Lentil Soup with Apple Smoked Bacon   Chocolate Velvet Cake

La Pergola

Blue Mountain Beach, Florida

"La Pergola" is the Italian word for an arbor, generally one under which a pathway exists. Pergolas are a common sight in towns and villages throughout Italy, and La Pergola is the pathway to the finest Mediterranean cuisine on the Gulf Coast. Positioned on a beautiful stretch of white sand in Santa Rosa Beach, our restaurant's view encompasses a stunning 180 degree span of the white sand and clear aqua waters of the Gulf. La Pergola beautifully unites its New World setting with a dedication to the Old World traditions of hospitality and quality, taking only the finest and freshest food available locally and infusing it with sunny Mediterranean spices.

Situated on what is traditionally known as the "Barbarossa" development, a Federal Land Grant Project of the 1940's, the site of La Pergola is historically rich and traces its foundation deep into legends of the Old World. Indeed, the name "Barbarossa" has well-documented and intriguing historical connections. In 1502, two brothers, both Christians, settled the area which is now known as Tunis in North Africa. From this strategic port settlement, just across the narrow inlet from the island of Sicily, Urue and Hizir Reis ruled the seas of the Mediterranean in the name of the Ottoman Empire. Upon Urue's premature death, Hizir became the premier naval commander of the Turkish navy and the highest ranking Admiral for Suleyman I the Magnificent, greatest Sultan of the Ottoman period.

Hizir sported a fiery red beard, leading the Christians who knew him to call him "Barbarossa," which in English means "red beard." Barbarossa's control of the Mediterranean involved many years along the Spanish coast. As Spain began to settle parts of the New World, Barbarossa's minions also spread out, bringing his influence all the way to Florida and to the Barbarossa Beach Club.

In honor of this rich history, La Pergola offers an authentic Mediterranean menu and wine list. Chef Jack Buchanan invites you to experience the flavors of the Mediterranean, enhanced by what he calls "a touch of Southern love." Originally from Gadsden, Alabama, Chef Buchanan was educated at Auburn University and trained at the Culinary Institute of America, the Hilton Corporation, and the Highlands Bar and Grill. He attributes his inspiration to a number of people: first, to his wife Luz Maria and his daughter Erika, and also to Joyce Jones, a high school instructor, and Shelby "Sam" Cochran, owner of "Mater's Pizza."

Destin Triggerfish
with Lump Crab and Caper Meuniere

"This dish has a great combination of texture and flavor."

2 ounces clarified butter
7-8 ounces Triggerfish portions
Salt, to taste
Pepper, to taste
2 ounces white wine

1 shallot, minced
$^1/2$ fresh lemon
1 teaspoon capers
1 ounce jumbo lump crab
2 ounces butter, softened
Pinch fresh parsley, chopped

Heat a sauté pan. Add enough clarified butter to coat the bottom of the pan. Liberally season fish with salt and pepper. Place fish in pan and sauté on its side until golden brown. Flip fish over and sauté until cooked thoroughly. Remove from pan. Deglaze pan with white wine. Add shallots and reduce until almost dry. Squeeze lemon into mixture. Add capers and crab. Carefully whisk in softened butter. Add parsley last. Ladle this sauce over the fish. Serve this dish with polenta.

Serves 1

Stuffed Roasted Peppers

1 red bell pepper
1 gold bell pepper
1 teaspoon extra virgin olive oil
$^1/4$ teaspoon balsamic vinegar
1 anchovy filet, ground

4 large leaves fresh basil
1 ounce feta cheese, crumbled
Pinch of kosher salt
Pinch coarse ground fresh pepper

Place peppers on a sheet pan in 500 degree oven. Turn peppers every 10 minutes to ensure even roasting. The skin will begin to blister.

When the peppers have blackened on all sides, remove them and place in a bowl. Wrap tightly with plastic wrap. Let them cool thoroughly. When peppers are cooled, cut them in half lengthwise, peeling off the outer skin and removing seeds. Take the juices that have formed and mix with olive oil and vinegar. Lay the peppers flat and sprinkle with anchovy. Tear 2 leaves of basil onto that. Crumble the feta cheese on top. Season to taste. Roll the peppers, reforming them to resemble their original shape. Drizzle over with oil, vinegar, and pepper juices. Tear remaining basil and garnish.

Vine Ripened Tomato Le Caprese Salad with Mozzarella

1 beefsteak tomato
3 ounces fresh "buffalo" mozzarella
5 leaves fresh basil

Pinch of coarsely ground black pepper
$1/4$ teaspoon white wine vinegar
1 teaspoon extra virgin olive oil

Slice the tomato to about $1/4$-inch thickness and arrange on plate. Slice the mozzarella about the same width and layer it between the tomatoes. Arrange the basil between the layers of cheese and tomato. Season with pepper. Drizzle with olive oil and vinegar.

Serves 1

Lentil Soup with Apple Smoked Bacon

2 ounces small diced
  apple-smoked bacon
1 small carrot, diced (4 ounces)
1 small onion, diced (4 ounces)
1 stick celery, diced (2 ounces)
1 cup dried lentils

$1^1/2$ cups water
$1^1/2$ cups chicken stock
2 bay leaves
$1/4$ teaspoon crushed red pepper
3 sprigs fresh thyme
Salt, to taste

In a sauce pot on medium heat, sauté the apple smoked bacon until crisp. Remove from pot. Sauté the carrots, onion, and celery until soft. Add the lentils and mix together. Add the water and stock and bring to a boil. Reduce heat to a simmer. Add back the bacon, together with bay leaves, crushed red pepper, and thyme. Simmer until lentils are soft but still hold their shape. Pour through strainer and save liquid. Take half the lentil mixture and puree it. Add it back to the liquid lentil mixture. Season with salt and pepper.

Serves 4

Chocolate Velvet Cake

"Any type of fruit puree will complement this dessert. Chef Buchanan's favorite is raspberry."

2^1/2 pounds semi-sweet chocolate
6 ounces butter
5 large eggs, separated
2 ounces Creme de Casis

1 ounce Meyers dark rum
3 ounces dark Creme de Cacao
24 ounces heavy cream, whipped firm
2 ounces powdered sugar

Chop chocolate and butter into small pieces and melt together over double boiler. Separate eggs; allow whites to come to room temperature. Beat yolks; add them to Creme de Casis, Meyers rum, and Creme de Cacao. Whip cream until firm. Beat whites until firm; add to them the powdered sugar. Add melted chocolate mixture to yolk mixture and gently fold in egg whites. Fold in whipped cream. Pour into a 10" spring form pan. Allow to refrigerate 8 hours before serving.

Makes 1 cake (approximately 12 servings)

FISH STOCK
(Also See Soup & Stock Tips, pg. 127).

You should save any liquids that are left over from cooking fish. Boil them down to a manageable amount, strain, and freeze. Use this whenever you need a bouillon or fish stock. Once saved, you can use and reuse it because each time you cook you will be adding to it and boiling it constantly. Since this base gets richer and richer over time, you may want to eventually use it as a base for a fish chowder or as a bouillabaisse.

Fish-based soups, chowders, and gumbos will taste better if you use shells and bones when you prepare the fish stock. Shrimp and lobster shells and fish bones cooked in water will give you a rich stock base.

The liquids from canned fish and seafood are useful when you need a stock or want to enhance the flavor of another stock. These liquids freeze well.

When you make a fish stock or soup, use lean fish. Fattier fish (i.e., mackerel, fresh tuna, bluefish, shad salmon, and trout) usually give an unpleasant taste to soups and stocks. Also avoid using fish heads in preparing stock. In a word, yuck.

More tips on page 121.

Filet Mignon with Slippertail Lobster Sauce   Grilled Grouper with
Salsa and Feta Cheese   Sesame Crusted yellowfin Tuna   Rice Pilaf
Spicy Tomato Soup   Cream of Chicken Soup

Saltwater Grill

Panama City, Florida

The doors of Saltwater Grill opened to Panama City back in 1989. Since that time, guests at Saltwater Grill have enjoyed some of Florida's freshest Gulf seafood, professionally prepared and served by the restaurants owner and chef Billy Redd and his staff. Saltwater Grill offers an extensive wine list that was chosen by Chef Redd and his associates to compliment his style. Mr. Redd explains that, every day, his chefs are let loose to create at least three daily specials. These featured dishes always depend on the seasonal availability of fresh seafood and vegetables, and they are as close to scratch as you can get.

What never changes at Saltwater Grill is the restaurants devotion to quality food and service, a virtue that has been recognized in several national publications. Saltwater Grill's critical acclaim includes 6 stars from The *Evansville, Indiana Courier*; 4 stars from the *Bay Digest*; and 4 stars from the *Tallahassee Democrat*. Of the restaurants popular acclaim there is never any doubt. Just ask anyone in Panama City where they like to eat and chances are they'll respond "Saltwater Grill."

Chef Billy Redd graduated from the Culinary Arts School of Gulf Coast College. He has won numerous awards that testify to his creativity and culinary professionalism. These awards include a Gold Medal at Region 1 V.I.C.A. culinary competition, a Gold Medal for the State of Florida V.I.C.A. culinary competition, and a Fourth place finish at the National V.I.C.A. Hot Foods Competition. He also finds the time to win awards in his favorite hobby, ice carving.

Saltwater Grill's standards of excellence promise that you will enjoy the most carefully prepared dishes and the finest seafood and vegetables available. If you are looking for a meal that is made from scratch daily and full of Emerald Coast spirit, then look for the neon sign hovering above Highway 98 in Panama City.

Filet Mignon with Slippertail Lobster Sauce

"This dish is excellent served with our wild rice pilaf and fresh steamed vegetables. A good Pinot Noir is perfect with the beef and lobster combination."

Filet Mignon

>2 (8-ounce) filet mignon
>2 (3-ounce) slippertail lobster tail meat

Grill the filet mignon to desired doneness. While the filets are cooking, cook the lobster tail by either steaming or grilling it.

Reheat the lobster sauce. Top the filet with the lobster tail and smother both with the lobster sauce.

Serves 2

Lobster Sauce

>$^1/_4$ cup butter
>$^1/_4$ cup flour
>$^1/_2$ teaspoon Lawry's seasoning salt
>$^1/_4$ teaspoon white pepper
>
>2 cups milk
>$^1/_2$ cup white wine
>8 ounces Swiss cheese, grated
>3 ounces mushrooms, sliced
>$^1/_4$ cup green onion, diced

Make a roux with the butter and flour. Season with Lawry's and white pepper. Add the milk and cook until thickened, stirring constantly. Add wine, cheese, mushrooms, and green onions. Stir until the cheese is melted.

This sauce can be made ahead and refrigerated for 1-3 days. Be sure to reheat the sauce before serving.

Grilled Grouper with Salsa and Feta Cheese

"This dish is perfect with grilled new potatoes and crusty bread. Serve it with any good Sauvignon Blanc or Pinot Blanc."

8 ounce portions of fresh, bone less black grouper fillets
Saltwater Salsa (recipe below)
4-6 ounces feta cheese or other good goat cheese

Grill the grouper fillet until done. Put fillet on a serving plate and top with heated Saltwater salsa. Crumble feta cheese over top of fish and serve.

Saltwater Salsa

2 tablespoons bacon fat
2 teaspoons garlic, minced
1 teaspoon ground cumin
$1/8$ teaspoon cayenne pepper
8-10 drops Tabasco sauce

$1/2$ tablespoon oregano
2 cups whole tomatoes
$1/2$ tablespoon Creole seasoning
1 cup bell pepper, diced
1 bundle green onions, chopped

In a sauce pan, add all of the ingredients except the green onions and the bell peppers. Cook on medium high heat for 6-10 minutes. Add onion and bell pepper. Heat for 2 minutes. Remove from heat and cool.

Yield is variable

Sesame Crusted Yellowfin Tuna

"Once the ingredients are compiled, this recipe takes only a few minutes to prepare. It is perfect as a nice dinner at home or to entertain friends in your own kitchen. Either a red or a white wine would be equally appropriate. If you choose white, Saltwater Grill recommends a spicy wine like Riesling. For a red, we recommend a Merlot."

7-ounce portions yellowfin tuna filets, desired amount	1 teaspoon butter
Sesame oil	1 ounce sherry
1 jar white sesame seeds	2 ounces Tupelo or Orange Blossom honey
1 jar black sesame seeds	4 ounces heavy cream

Lightly oil the tuna fillets with a touch of sesame oil. Mix the white and black sesame seeds together and coat the tuna fillets with the sesame seeds.

In a 12-inch sauté pan, heat 1/2 ounce sesame oil and 1 teaspoon butter until almost smoking. Add the sesame coated tuna fillets to the hot pan carefully to avoid splattering. Sear the fillets on both sides for approximately 2 minutes on each side.

Deglaze pan with 1 ounce sherry and remove the tuna fillets to a serving plate. Add 2 ounces honey and 4 ounces heavy cream to the pan and heat until thickened (about 2 minutes). Top the tuna fillets with the sauce and enjoy!

Yield is variable

Rice Pilaf

5 1/2 cups hot water	1 cup onion, diced small
5 tablespoons chicken base	1 teaspoon white pepper
1/2 cup butter	3 cups converted rice
1 cup red bell pepper, diced small	1 cup wild rice, cooked
2 cups carrots, diced small	2 tablespoons Cavender's Greek seasoning
1 cup celery, diced small	1 tablespoon salt
1 1/2 cups mushrooms, sliced	

Combine the hot water and the chicken base to make a chicken stock. Make this stock in advance and keep it very hot.

Melt butter in sauce pan. Add the vegetables and sauté until the onions are opaque and carrots are tender. Add the rice and stir well to coat each individual grain. Add the spices. Pour the hot stock in with the rice. Bring to a boil, reduce heat, and cover for 20 minutes or until the rice is done. Fluff rice with a fork before serving with entree.

Serves 6

Spicy Tomato Soup

"We have always found that garlic croutons and grated Parmesan cheese are a nice garnish for the spicy tomato soup."

2 bunches green onions, chopped
2 large green bell peppers, diced
2 tablespoons bacon fat
1 (10-pound) can whole tomatoes
4 cups V-8 juice
2 tablespoons beef base
1 tablespoon basil

1 tablespoon oregano
1 tablespoon cumin, ground
2 teaspoons paprika
1^1/2 tablespoons garlic, minced
2 teaspoons celery seed
Approx. 4 cups white sauce
   (recipe below)
1 teaspoon white pepper

In a stock pot, sauté the peppers and onions in the bacon grease. Add the tomatoes, juice, and beef base and bring to a boil. Add the spices and simmer for 15 minutes. When cooked, puree the mixture and whisk in the white sauce (recipe below).

White Sauce

^{1}/2 cup flour
^{1}/2 cup butter
3 cups whipping cream

Blend all ingredients until smooth. Use this as the base for the spicy tomato soup.

Cream of Chicken a la Reine Soup

"It's nice to have some cooked, shredded chicken breast meat on hand to garnish the soup when you serve it."

8 ounces celery, diced
8 ounces onion, diced
2¹/2 ounces butter
2 ounces flour
1¹/2 quarts chicken stock, hot
1 bay leaf

8 ounces chicken breast
1 pint half & half
Salt, to taste
Pepper, to taste
Fresh parsley, chopped

Sauté celery and onion in butter until translucent. Add flour to make a roux. Cook for 5 minutes over low heat and add hot chicken stock. Whip vigorously in order to incorporate. Add bay leaf and simmer for 20 minutes. Chop chicken into fine pieces and add to soup, simmer for 10 minutes. Temper in the half and half, adjusting seasonings to taste. Remove the bay leaf. Serve soup garnished with chopped parsley.

HINTS AND TIPS

SHRIMP & CRAB

When boiling peeled shrimp, wash the shells that you removed and put them in water. Bring the water to a boil and let the shells simmer for a few minutes. Strain this liquid and use it for cooking your shrimp. They will have a richer flavor.

Shrimp takes on a lobster-like flavor if you simmer them, unpeeled, in beer.

If you are going to serve cold shrimp, remove them from the water when they are cooked and let them cool gradually at room temperature. They will have a tougher texture if you refrigerate them before they have cooled gradually.

1 pound of cooked crabmeat equals 2 cups.

You should soak canned crabmeat and any othet kind of canned seafood in very cold water for a short time to remove the canned flavor it usually has.

RICE

For whiter, brighter rice, squeeze the juice of a fresh lemon into the water in which you will boil the rice.

Enhance your plain white rice with a little white wine, Marsala, or sherry. Combine the uncooked rice with some melted butter and one of the above, add your liquid, and cook.

PASTA

Pasta doubles in volume when you cook it.

Adding a tablespoon of oil to the water in which you boil pasta will keep it from sticking together and will also keep the water from boiling over the sides of the pot.

When boiling pasta, add 1 teaspoon salt to the water. Cooked pasta that tastes very faintly salty works better with the sauces and cheeses that may cover it.

More tips on page 127

Snapper Amaretto   Chicken Cacciotore   Shrimp Genoa   Veal Scotto
Baked Snapper Ricotta

Scotto's Ristorante Italiano

Pensacola, Florida

Located in one of the Emerald Coast's oldest and most captivating regions, the Seville Square district of Pensacola, Scotto's Ristorante Italiano recaptures the ambiance and hospitality of gracious dining traditions of the past. Housed in a charming and historic home built in the late 1800's, Scotto's can be found on the corner of Alcaniz and Government Streets.

Operated by Pat and Richard Scotto, Scotto's is steeped in family heritage and Italian tradition. When you enter Scotto's, you will step into an elegant 1930's style atmosphere where the walls are adorned with classic family portraits and the sounds of authentic Italian music fill the dining room.

Flanking the family portraits are photos of second son Guiseppe "Pappa Joe" Scotto in his early 20's. These cherished photographs provide the basis of the distinctive Scotto logo.

At Scotto's, we use only the finest and freshest ingredients in our cooking, and all of our pasta is handmade fresh daily in our kitchen. When at Scotto's, we encourage you to try Richard's own Ultimate Cheesecake, which, like Scotto's restaurant itself, is a true Pensacola favorite

Because it is a family-run restaurant, Scotto's imparts an unparalleled sense of comfort, pleasure, and satisfaction. Making guests comfortable and serving the most authentic Italian cuisine in Pensacola are goals to which the Scotto family is devoted. When in the Emerald Coast, visit Scotto's and discover for yourself the restaurant that has delighted Pensacola for more than ten years.

Snapper Amaretto

"Snapper Amaretto is one of Scotto's house specialties. It is a wonderful dish for festive occasions."

Olive oil
2 (8-ounce) snapper filets
$1/2$ cup Amaretto di Saionne
$1^1/2$ cups heavy whipping cream
2 cups roasted almonds

Line the bottom of a large baking dish with olive oil and top with snapper filets. Broil for approximately 10 minutes.

In a large heated saucepan, reduce the Amaretto. Add heavy whipping cream and reduce by half. Remove from heat.

Transfer snapper filets to a platter and keep warm. Cover filets with almonds and drizzle Amaretto sauce over the top. Serve immediately.

Serves 2

Chicken Cacciotore

"An old Italian standard that we prepare in our kitchen daily. Chianti wine is a terrific compliment to this dish."

2 large chicken breasts
3 tablespoons extra virgin olive oil
$1/8$ cup chicken stock
$1/2$ cup onion, diced
$1/2$ medium green bell pepper, cut finely

$1/2$ cup mushrooms, sliced
$1/8$ cup black olives, diced
3 cloves garlic, minced
$1/4$ tablespoon oregano
3 ounces red wine

Brown chicken in olive oil. Add stock, onions, and green peppers and simmer for 5 minutes. Add remaining ingredients. Cook uncovered on medium heat until the chicken is tender. If sauce thickens too quickly, add $1/2$ cup of water. When chicken is done and sauce is thickened, serve immediately over linguine cooked al dente.

Serves 2

Shrimp Genoa

"A perfect way to prepare fresh Gulf shrimp"

$1/4$ cup of extra virgin olive oil
1 pound fresh shrimp, peeled and deveined
3 cloves garlic, minced
2 cups tomatoes, diced

Fresh parsley, chopped
2 tablespoons capers
1 pound angel hair pasta, cooked
$1/4$ cup fontina cheese

Heat olive oil in sauté pan. Add shrimp and garlic. Cook until the shrimp turn pink and begin to curl. Add tomatoes, parsley, and capers. Briefly simmer over low heat. Transfer hot angel hair pasta to a serving platter. Pour shrimp over pasta and sprinkle fontina cheese over the top. Serve immediately.

Serves 4

Veal Scotto

"Veal Scotto is a menu favorite. A Merlot wine is a perfect accompaniment."

1 pound veal scaloppine, very
  thinly sliced and pounded flat
Flour, for dusting
2 tablespoons olive oil
2 tablespoons butter
Red wine
$1^{1}/2$ cups heavy whipping cream
$1/2$ cup beef broth

$1/4$ medium bell pepper, sliced thinly
$1/8$ cup onions, diced
$1/4$ cup fresh mushrooms, sliced
$1/4$ cup tomatoes, chopped
4 black olives, sliced
4 broccoli florettes, chopped
2 artichoke hearts, quartered
4 spears asparagus

Lightly dust the veal scaloppine with flour. In a large saucepan, heat the olive oil and butter and sauté the lightly floured veal on both sides. Remove from pan.

Deglaze pan with red wine. Add cream and reduce by half. Add remaining ingredients and cook until the vegetables are tender. When the sauce thickens, turn heat down to low and add veal scaloppine, turning and basting them with mixture once or twice. Transfer meat and sauce to a warm platter and serve immediately.

Serves 2

Baked Snapper Ricotta

2 tablespoons butter
1 large green onion, finely chopped
1 clove garlic, minced
$^3/_4$ cup ricotta cheese
1 egg, lightly beaten
$1^1/_2$ teaspoons fresh parsley,
  finely chopped
$1^1/_2$ teaspoons fresh thyme,
finely minced

Salt, to taste
Freshly ground pepper, to taste
1 pound snapper, cut into 8 pieces
8 slices ripe tomato, $^1/_4$" thick
2 tablespoons butter, melted
Juice from $^1/_4$ lemon
12 ounces mozzarella cheese, shredded
Paprika
Fresh parsley, chopped

Melt butter in a small skillet over medium heat. Add onion and saute'. Add garlic and saute' for an additional minute. Remove from heat.

In a small bowl, combine ricotta, egg, and parsley. Add onion and garlic mixture. Season with thyme and salt and pepper to taste. Cover and refrigerate for 1 hour.

Arrange half the snapper filets in lightly buttered baking dish in a single layer. Spread ricotta mixture evenly over the filets. Top with remaining filets. Place 2 tomato slices on each portion. Brush lightly with melted butter and sprinkle with salt and pepper. Squeeze lemon juice over all.

Bake in a 350 degree oven for 15 to 20 minutes until fish is almost done. Sprinkle the mozzarella cheese and then paprika over the filets and continue baking for 5 minutes or until cheese melts. Garnish with parsley.

serves 2

Hints and Tips

Soup and Stock

The water and juices from cooked and canned vegetables and mushrooms improves the flavor of soup. You can freeze these liquids until you are ready to use them.

To make an amazing stock, you will need the bones and carcasses for the beef, pork, chicken, fish, etc. Many people feel that boiling a pot full of bones, carcasses, and other "leftovers" is a grotesque as it is unappealing, but there is simply no other way to create a rich, honest, and flavorful stock. If you are accustomed to canned stocks and bouillons, you'll be amazed at the difference that a stock simply prepared from scratch makes.

Put soup bones and meat in cold salted water and bring to a boil. Doing this will extract a lot more flavor from the bones than if you were to throw them into already boiling water.

Meat or vegetables first browned in a hot oven will give a soup or stock a much heartier and richer winter or autumn-like flavor.

Fruits, Vegetables, and Seasonings

If you are cooking something with the intention of freezing it for later use, avoid seasoning it. The flavor and potency of most herbs and spices dies in the freezer. Instead, add the necessary seasonings whenever you reheat the frozen food.

Whenever possible, gently scrub all fresh fruits in warm, soapy water before eating them. Unfortunately, they are usually coated with insecticides, decay inhibitors, waxes, and/or dyes when you buy them. Gross, huh?

Use a mortar and pestle to grind your spices and garlic before cooking with them. Even if you are using dried herbs, crushing them in a mortar reawakens their flavor and potency.

Aunt Aggie's Original Scalloped Oysters   Staff's Original Tartar Sauce
Staff's Original Thousand Island Dressing   Aunt Aggie's Apple Pie

Staff's Seafood Restaurant

Fort Walton Beach, Florida

The spirit of Staff's cooking lies in an 80 year-old family tradition of serving scores of vacationing guests. Staff's prepares each meal as though family and guests are arriving for dinner, using only natural ingredients that are not doused with preservatives or flavor enhancers. Nothing at Staff's is pre-breaded, institutionally proportioned, frozen, or in other ways pre-prepared, and all of the produce is bought fresh from the market each day. Not only do Staff's meals taste good, they are good for you -- carefully prepared with conscience and a concern for low fat and low cholesterol diets.

The Staff family history and the evolution of Fort Walton Beach's favorite restaurant are equally intriguing. Mexico, 1912: Theodore Staff and his family had a healthy life on their plantation in the tropics south of Mexico City. It was a utopian lifestyle for the Staff family, but as history unrolled, the Staffs began to feel the pressures of the Mexican revolutionary, Pancho Villa, and his anti-foreign campaign. During this time, Mexican banditos raided and pillaged "gringo" communities, forcing many Americans to hide in the jungle as their property and possessions were stolen or destroyed. Luckily, Theo and his wife Molly and their children evacuated Mexico safely, settling in what was once known as Camp Walton, a small outpost in northwest Florida with a population of 90.

In 1912, Theo purchased a large lodging facility on the shores of Camp Walton and opened the Gulfview Hotel. Tourism then comprised of a few weary travelers who trekked from Montgomery and Birmingham to Pensacola by train and then by small boat to the docks of the Gulfview Hotel.

To accommodate the steadily growing number of guests at the Gulfview, the family opened Staff's Restaurant. Theodore "Docie" Bass, who married Theo and Molly Staff's daughter Aggie, expanded the family recipes in order to feed the crowds. Staff's present menu has many of the historic items that Docie originated, but the sauces and methods of preparation have been refined in order to adapt with popular trends and tastes.

Today, the restaurant is still operated by the Staff and Bass clans, and some of the recipes were submitted to us on old paper in Aunt Aggie's handwriting. True family keepsakes, these recipes were some of Aunt Aggie's personal favorites. Staff's also presents its original Tartar Sauce and Thousand Island dressing. (In the 1940's, a Kraft Company representative requested Staff's recipe for the Thousand Island dressing, which was unknown to the world then. Shortly after, Kraft copied the recipe, bottled it, and turned it into a national favorite.)

From Mexico to Fort Walton Beach, this spirited family has wound its way through life's turmoil. Their faith in God and the goodness of those with courage marks them as witness to an era in which hard work, integrity, and honesty were the guidelines of human service and contentment. Today, you will find these same principles at work when you visit Staff's restaurant. Their legendary good food and the good people who serve it continue on, undiminished.

Aunt Aggie's Original Scalloped Oysters

"This is the family's favorite side dish when they gather at Thanksgiving and Christmas. Try this with your regular dressing or stuffing."

2 sticks butter*
3 large onions, finely cut
1 pint canned sliced mushrooms
Salt, to taste
Pepper, to taste
2 quarts large oysters

2 tablespoons sifted flour
$1/4$ pint light cream
$1/2$ quart sweet milk
1 large loaf fresh French bread
$1/4$ pound bacon

* Margarine may be substituted for butter. However, when Aunt Aggie made this, margarine was not yet invented.

Melt half a stick of butter in a large frying pan. Add onions and fry until slightly brown. Add mushrooms. Salt and pepper to taste.

Drain liquid from oysters, saving liquid for later use. Put oysters in a large boiler and bring to a rapid boil. Remove from heat when oysters are plump.

In a separate boiler, melt 1 stick of butter. To melted butter, add the sifted flour, stirring constantly so that no lumps form. Add to this the cream, oyster liquid, and the sweet milk. Cook until smooth.

Combine this sauce with the onions and mushrooms and put over the oysters. Bring to a boil.

Crumble the French bread into fine crumbs. Brown in oven. Melt $1/2$ stick of butter and pour over bread crumbs.

Arrange in a large casserole by making a layer of crumbs and a layer of oysters, ending with bread crumbs on the top layer. Fry bacon until crisp and crumble on top of casserole. Bake in 350 degree oven for 30 minutes.

Serves 10

Staff's Original Tartar Sauce

"No decent fried seafood should be served without this tartar sauce. It's still the number one choice for shrimp that is seasoned, battered, and fried to a golden brown. Expand your horizons! Also try some tartar sauce with onion rings or French fries."

12 large onions, chopped
1/2 gallon sweet relish, drained
1/2 gallon dill relish, drained
21 ounces capers, chopped and drained
4 ounces real lemon juice
4 gallons mayonnaise

Mix all ingredients in a large pan or bowl. Store in jars at 34 degrees.
Makes 5 1/3 gallons

Staff's Original Thousand Island Dressing

"Although not as popular as Ranch dressing these days, Thousand Island can still bring out the taste of salad like nothing else. Use this along with other dips on your next vegetable tray at a party. Try it again for the first time."

1 (10-pound) can chili sauce
2 gallons mayonnaise
1 (5-ounce) bottle Lea
  and Perrins sauce
1/2 gallon dill relish, drained
1/2 gallon sweet relish, drained

Mix all ingredients together in a large bowl. Store in jars at 34 degrees.

Aunt Aggie's Apple Pie

"The all-time American favorite as an ending to any meal. Always great with seafood, pork, lamb, or beef. Aunt Aggie made this frequently because it was the perfect thing to serve when her friends and family stopped by for afternoon coffee."

Pastry

> **2 cups flour**
> **1 teaspoon salt**
> **³/4 cup Wesson oil**
> **¹/4 cup milk**

Sift flour and salt. Add Wesson oil mixed with milk. Stir at once with a fork until well mixed. Roll out half of dough between two sheets of wax paper. Peel off top sheet of paper and turn pastry onto pie plate.

Filling

> **4 large apples, peeled**
> **1 cup sugar**
> **1 tablespoon lemon juice**
> **2 tablespoons butter**
> **Dash of cinnamon**
> **Dash of nutmeg**

Slice apples into pie plate. Add sugar, lemon juice, butter, and spices. Roll out remaining pastry and cover apples. Bake at 375 degrees for half an hour. Lower oven temperature to 350 degrees and bake for an additional half hour.

Makes 1 pie (6-8 servings)

Recipe
Notes

Sunset Spinach Fettucine   Blackened Grouper with Creole Hollandaise
Sunset Bay Jambalaya   Beef Carpachio   Mustard Lamb Shanks   Potato Galette with Roasted
Peppers and Cheese   Sunset Bay Seafood Gumbo   Trivoli Cream Brulee   Five Star Bread
Pudding with Butter Rum Sauce   Sandestin Derby Pie   Banana Rum Cheesecake
Ultimate Flourless Cake   Bubba's Au Rum

Sunset Bay Cafe

Sandestin, Florida

Sunset Bay Cafe is Sandestin's family grille. Sitting directly on Choctawhatchee Bay, the Caribbean-themed restaurant features both a spectacular view and an eclectic menu reminiscent of the islands. Magnificently exemplifying the sheer artistry and perfection that characterizes all of Sandestin resort, Sunset Bay Cafe is a remarkable restaurant, awash with style and some of the Emerald Coasts' most enticing cuisine.

Sunset Bay Cafe is also a trend setting restaurant, thanks to the expertise and creativity of the chefs and management. In addition to offering popular items such as burgers, pasta, seafood, and its award-winning gumbo, Sunset Bay includes many Heart Healthy selections on the menu, which the chefs prepare with a conscience for nutrition and good health. And, the newest sensation at Sunset Bay, called Hot Rock cooking, features shrimp, beef, or chicken prepared over a fiery volcanic rock at your table.

Sunset Bay is captivating and exciting in every way. No wonder it remains a true Emerald Coast favorite -- a restaurant where you can fully experience the finest Gulf-fresh food and the tropical flavor of the Caribbean islands. With the recipes in this section, you can now experience some of this magic in your own kitchen. Or when you are in the area, stop in for a culinary adventure that you will never forget. Sunset Bay Cafe serves breakfast, lunch, and dinner seven days a week. Take out and delivery are also available.

Sunset Spinach Fettucine

"A longtime favorite from the Caribbean."

3 ounces light tomato sauce*
3 tablespoons sundried tomatoes, diced
1/2 tablespoon cilantro, chopped
1 teaspoon garlic, finely minced

1³/4 cups spinach fettucine, cooked
1¹/2 ounces heavy whipping cream
1 grilled chicken breast, sliced
   (or) 21-25 grilled shrimp

* *You may use any spaghetti or marinara sauce, preferably without meat.*

In a sauté pan, sauté tomato sauce, sundried tomatoes, cilantro, and garlic. Dip spinach fettucine in hot water for 15-20 seconds. Drain well. Add heavy whipping cream and pasta to sauce pan. Place in pasta bowl and top with sliced chicken breast or shrimp.

Serves 1

Blackened Grouper with Creole Hollandaise

"One of Southern Louisiana's finest foods."

Blackened Grouper

16 ounces fresh grouper filets
1 ounce blackening spice (see Elephant Walk recipe)
Creole Hollandaise (recipe below)

Coat fish in blackening spice. Cook in a sauté pan until brown on both sides and remove from pan. Place fish in hot oven and finish cooking. Top with Creole Hollandaise.

Creole Hollandaise

2 egg yolks
1 ounce white wine
3 ounces drawn butter
1/4 ounce Tabasco

1/8 ounce Worcestershire
Dash white pepper
Dash salt
1/2 ounce Creole mustard

In a stainless steel mixing bowl, whisk egg yolks and white wine over steam bath until color changes. Remove from heat and slowly add warm (150 degree) butter. Season with remaining ingredients.

Serves 2

Sunset Bay Jambalaya

"Our own rendition of this Creole favorite."

1 pound diced bacon
1/3 pound diced Andouille sausage
2 medium onions, diced
1/8 cup minced garlic
2 medium green peppers, diced
1 bay leaf
1/2 teaspoon thyme
2 cups uncooked white rice
2 tablespoons tomato paste

2 cups fresh tomatoes, chopped
1/2 cup celery, chopped
1/4 cup parsley, chopped
2 teaspoons salt
1/2 teaspoon black pepper
Cayenne pepper, to taste
46 ounces clam juice
2 pounds roasted or grilled
  chicken, chopped
1/2 pound cooked black beans

Cook bacon until crisp. Add Andouille sausage and sauté for 2 minutes. Add onions, garlic, green peppers, bay leaf, and thyme. Sauté for 5 minutes. Add rice and sauté for 3 minutes, stirring constantly. Add tomato paste and cook for another 3 minutes. Add tomatoes, celery, parsley, salt, pepper, cayenne pepper, and clam juice. Bring to a boil and reduce heat. Cook slowly until rice is done. Toss in cooked chicken and black beans at serving time.

Beef Carpachio

"A fine summer appetizer"

1 teaspoon olive oil
2 (8-ounce) filets of beef tenderloin
1/2 cup fresh crushed black pepper
2 large tomatoes, diced

1 tablespoon fresh basil,
  chopped
2 cloves fresh garlic, minced
2 tablespoons extra virgin olive oil
Salt, to taste

Place sauté pan with 1 teaspoon olive oil on high heat. Coat filets with pepper. Place them in a pan and sear the exterior of the filets; do not fully cook. Remove filets from heat. Wrap in foil and chill. When chilled, slice filets 1/4" against the grain, and arrange on a platter in a circular fashion.

Mix tomatoes, basil, and garlic with 2 tablespoons olive oil and salt to taste. Place tomato mixture in center of the plated meat.

Serves 4

Mustard Lamb Shanks

"The flavor in this cut of lamb is unbelievable."

4 lamb hind shanks
1 head garlic, roughly chopped
1 onion, roughly chopped
1 carrot, roughly chopped
Chicken stock, enough to cover
   3/4 of the lamb

1 1/2 cups whole grain mustard
1 teaspoon fresh Rosemary
Salt, to taste
Pepper, to taste

Preheat oven to 350 degrees. In a large sauté pan on medium to high heat, sear the shanks until golden brown on all sides. Add garlic, onion, and carrot and brown slightly. Cover 3/4 with chicken stock. Add one cup of mustard and the fresh rosemary. Bring to a simmer and cover with aluminum foil. Place in oven for one hour or until tender.

Strain off sauce, saving the liquid. Reduce liquid over high heat until proper consistency and add remaining mustard.

Season with salt and pepper. Arrange shanks on a platter and cover them with the finished sauce.

Potato Galette with Roasted Peppers and Cheese

"This dish is a fine complement to any meal."

5 (8-ounce) potatoes,
   peeled and thinly sliced
1 teaspoon salt
1 teaspoon black pepper
Butter
2 red bell peppers, roasted and julienned

3 cups Gruyere cheese, grated
1 cup goat cheese, crumbled
2 teaspoons Herbes de Provence
3 cloves garlic, minced
2 1/2 cups milk
1 egg, beaten

Toss thinly-sliced potatoes with salt and pepper. Thickly butter a 12" round cast iron skillet. Overlap potatoes in a circular pattern. Combine peppers, cheeses, herbs, and garlic and top potatoes with a third of this mixture. Cover with another layer of potatoes. Cover again with the remaining pepper and cheese mixture.

Heat milk and add beaten egg. Pour over potatoes and bake at 400 degrees for 45-60 minutes. Let cool for 10 minutes. Cut into wedges and serve with your favorite mixed greens and vinaigrette.

Sunset Bay Seafood Gumbo

"This dish was the Peoples Choice winner in the Great Southern Gumbo Cookoff 1993 and 1994."

2 pounds Andouille Sausage, diced
3/5 cup fresh garlic, chopped
1/4 bottle Jack Daniels
2 onions, chopped
2 red peppers, chopped
2 green peppers, chopped
4 stalks celery, chopped
2 cans clam juice
1 quart canned tomatoes
3/4 gallon water
1/4 gallon red wine
3 teaspoons dried oregano
2 teaspoons dried thyme
1 teaspoon white pepper
1 teaspoon black pepper

1/2 teaspoon cayenne pepper
1 teaspoon cumin
1 tablespoon gumbo file (ground sassafras leaves)
1/2 cup Worcestershire sauce
1/4 cup Durkee Red Hot Sauce
2 ounces chicken bouillon
2 ounces lobster bouillon
2 ounces clam bouillon
2 ounces shrimp bouillon
Dark brown roux (use salad or olive oil rather than butter, which will burn as the roux darkens.)
1 bag (32 ounces) frozen okra
1/2 tablespoon salt

Cook sausage until slightly brown. Add garlic and brown slightly. Deglaze with Jack Daniels. Add onions, peppers, celery. Sauté lightly. Add clam juice, tomatoes, water, and red wine. Add all spices. Add all sauces and bases (bouillon). Add dark brown roux and cook until desired thickness. (It takes only 30 minutes for the roux to cook out completely.) Add okra and salt to taste if necessary.

Makes 2 gallons or 32 servings

Note: leftover gumbo can be frozen after being properly cooled. If the seafood bouillons are not commercially available, they can be prepared as any other stock by boiling the base ingredient and reducing the liquid.

Tivoli Cream Brulee

"This dessert makes you think you are in heaven."

1 cup half and half	1^1/2 cups sugar
1 vanilla bean	1 quart heavy cream
16 egg yolks	4 ounces chocolate shavings

Bring half & half to a boil. Add vanilla bean.

Slightly whip egg yolks and sugar. Stirring continuously, temper* the yolk mixture by adding just enough hot half to warm yolks up to near the temperature of the hot half and half. Take this mixture and add it to the remaining hot half and half. Strain yolk mixture into heavy cream, stirring until incorporated.

Place 1 tablespoon chocolate shavings into each mold. Add 6 ounces of brulee batter to each mold. Bake at 350 degrees for 18 minutes.

* Temper: adding small amounts of hot liquid to large amounts of hot or room temperature liquid until it becomes hot.

Serves 8

Five Star Bread Pudding with Butter Rum Sauce

"This is the finest bread pudding you will ever eat."

Bread slices	3 cans sweetened condensed milk
3 cups water	6 eggs, slightly beaten
2 sticks butter	2 teaspoons vanilla
3 ounces raisins	Cinnamon

Butter a 9 x 10^1/2" pan. Slice bread into 1-inch cubes and fill pan to three quarters full with cubed bread.

In a pan, heat water and butter until butter is melted completely. Add raisins. Stir sweetened condensed milk into butter mixture and let cool slightly. Add eggs and vanilla to mixture and pour over bread, letting it soak. Sprinkle the top of the bread with cinnamon and bake at 350 degrees for 40 minutes. Serve topped with Butter Rum Sauce (next page)

Butter Rum Sauce

> 1 cup sugar
> 2 cups water
> 4 ounces rum
> 4 ounces butter

Heat sugar and water to 230 degrees. Add rum. Let cool to 120 degrees and add butter.

Sandestin Derby Pie

"For all the chocolate and nut lovers"

Crust

> 1$1/4$ cups all purpose flour
> $1/2$ teaspoon salt
> $1/8$ teaspoon cinnamon
> 1 stick unsalted butter, cut into small pieces
> $1/4$ cup ice water

Blend flour, salt, and cinnamon in a bowl. Place butter into flour mixture. With a pastry cutter, cut butter until mixture forms lumps the size of a pea. Add ice water to mixture and mix until it comes together. Chill for 1/2 hour and roll into a 9-inch pie tin.

Filling

> 1 stick margarine
> 2 eggs, slightly beaten
> $1/2$ cup all-purpose flour
> 1 teaspoon vanilla
> 1 cup pecans
> 1 cup semi-sweet chocolate

Blend first 4 ingredients together, then stir in pecans and chocolate chips. Pour into unbaked 9" pie shell. Bake at 325 degrees for 1 hour.

Banana Rum Cheesecake

"Sandestin's original recipe that people have been trying to duplicate for years."

Crust

> **3 cups graham cracker crumbs**
> **$1/2$ cup melted butter or margarine**

Mix both ingredients. Place in spring form pan to form a 1/8-inch crust along the bottom.

Filling

> **Pinch of salt**
> **$1^3/4$ cups sugar**
> **2 pounds cream cheese**
> **5 whole eggs**
> **4 egg yolks**

> **1 ounce corn starch**
> **3 tablespoons dark rum**
> **3 tablespoons light rum**
> **2 bananas**

In a mixing bowl, cream the salt, sugar, and cream cheese until smooth. Incorporate whole eggs and egg yolks one at a time into cream cheese mixture.

In a separate bowl, mix the corn starch, rum, and bananas together until smooth. Fold banana mixture into cheese mixture. Place mixture in the spring form pan with the graham cracker crust. Bake at 350 degrees in water bath for $1^1/2$ hours. Cool before removing from spring pan. Top with Dark Rum Sauce (recipe below).

Dark Rum Sauce

> **8 ounces corn syrup**
> **4 ounces water**
> **2 ounces dark rum**

Place corn syrup and water in sauce pan and bring to a boil. Take pan off stove and add dark rum.

Makes 1 cake

Ultimate Flourless Cake

"This dessert melts in your mouth!"

9 ounces dark bittersweet
    chocolate
4^1/2 ounces butter
9 egg yolks

^{2}/3 cup sugar
9 egg whites
Ganache coating (recipe below)

Warm chocolate and butter to 110 degrees until lump free. Whip egg yolks and ^{1}/3 cup sugar for 12 minutes. Whip egg whites and ^{1}/3 cup sugar until soft peaks form. Fold chocolate into egg yolks. Fold egg whites into chocolate mixture.

Place mixture in a 9" cake pan lined with wax paper. Bake at 350 degrees for 35 minutes. Upon cooling, the cake will fall into the pan -- this is normal. Take the cake out of the pan and level with a knife. Flip cake upside down and coat with ganache (recipe below).

Ganache Coating

8 ounces dark bittersweet chocolate
1 cup cream

Bring cream to a boil. Remove from heat and stir in chocolate until smooth.

Makes 1 (9-inch) cake

Bubba's Au Rum

"This recipe was perfected in France years ago."

6 eggs
2 packages dry active yeast
17 ounces high gluten flour
1^1/2 teaspoons salt

1 tablespoon water
6 ounces butter
Rum sauce (recipe below)

Warm eggs to 90 degrees over double boiler and add dry active yeast. Place flour, eggs, yeast, and salt into a mixing bowl and mix on second speed for 10 minutes (if mixture is too dry, add the tablespoon of water.) Add butter to batter and mix slightly. Set aside and let rise until double in size. Put mixture into 12 well greased molds and fill each ^{1}/2 way. Bake at 350 degrees until knife inserted in the middle comes out clean. Top each with rum sauce.

Rum Sauce

1 pint water
1^1/2 cups sugar
^{3}/4 cup rum
1 tablespoon orange zest

Bring water and sugar to a boil. Add rum and orange zest.

Serves 12

Recipe
Notes

Chicken Marsala   Chicken Cacciatore   Scampi Provencal
Seafood Fettucine

Sweet Basil's Bistro

3 locations: Panama City Beach, Florida / Destin, Florida
New Orleans, Louisiana

Sweet Basil's Bistro is a sterling example of how the Emerald Coast benefits from its lucky proximity to New Orleans. The original Sweet Basil's, a famous New Orleans tradition, has for many years gifted the Emerald Coast with the openings of two additional restaurants in Panama City and Destin. Now Northwest Florida can enjoy Sweet Basil's famous Italian cuisine without driving hours west to Louisiana.

Sweet Basil's has been serving a touch of Italy to the Emerald Coast for more than five years. Owner Gerald Senner has brought together authentic Italian recipes and chefs dedicated to preserving the rich tradition of Italian cuisine. The results of these efforts have proven award winning. From the creamy flavor of real Romano in our alfredo to the zesty taste of pesto in our dressing, each of our entrees provides a culinary delight. In fact, Sweet Basil's has so successfully captured the spirit of Italian cuisine that it enjoys one of the most highly-regarded and extensive reputations in the Emerald Coast.

We at Sweet Basil's invite you to enjoy the tastes of Italy served in a relaxing, casual atmosphere. Join us at either of our Emerald Coast locations or at our original location in New Orleans. But if you are not in the area, try preparing some of our delicious Italian dishes in your own kitchen.

Chicken Marsala

"Serve with a Brolio Chianti Classico."

1 (8-ounce) chicken breast	Pinch of pepper
1 ounce olive oil	Pinch of minced garlic
$^1/_2$ cup mushrooms	2 ounces butter
Pinch of onion, chopped	1 tablespoon lemon juice
Pinch of salt	2 ounces Marsala wine

Grill chicken breast until thoroughly cooked. Heat olive oil in sauté pan and add mushrooms, onions, and spices. Deglaze with Marsala wine. Add butter and lemon juice. Simmer until sauce begins to thicken. Remove from heat and pour over grilled chicken breast. Serve with fettuccine alfredo.

Serves 1

Chicken Cacciatore

"Chicken Cacciatore goes well with a Bolla Valpolicella."

2 ounces green peppers, diced	$^1/_2$ teaspoon black pepper
2 ounces onion, diced	1 bay leaf
1 ounce celery, diced	6 ounces marinara sauce
Olive oil	4 ounces chicken breast, diced
1 tablespoon garlic, minced	5 ounces capellini
2 tablespoons sugar	

Blanch peppers in hot water. Sauté onions and celery in a small amount of olive oil. Add peppers, sugar, and all spices. Add marinara sauce and simmer for 15 minutes. While sauce is simmering, lightly dust chicken in flour and sauté in a small amount of olive oil. Add chicken to sauce and pour over capellini.

Serves 1

Scampi Provencal

"If you are looking for a nice wine to complement this dish, try a Torresella Pinot Grigio."

7 shrimp, peeled and deveined
1 ounce olive oil
Pinch onion, garlic, black pepper,
   salt, seafood seasoning, and basil
2 ounces tomato filets

2 ounces white wine
1/4 cup green onions
1 tablespoon lemon juice
2 ounces butter
5 ounces capellini, cooked

Heat olive oil in sauté pan. Add shrimp and sauté until 75% done. Deglaze with white wine. As wine begins to boil, add butter and lemon juice. Add tomato filets, onion, and spices. Allow to simmer only until sauce begins to thicken. Remove and spoon over capellini.

Serves 1

Seafood Fettucine

"A Glen Ellen Chardonnay is a good choice to serve with this dish."

10 ounces fresh snapper
4 ounces shrimp
Olive oil
8 ounces crab meat
1/4 cup onion, chopped
1 tablespoon basil
1 teaspoon oregano

1 teaspoon black pepper
1 teaspoon seafood base
1 tablespoon garlic, minced
8 ounces alfredo sauce
12 ounces fettucine, cooked

Sauté snapper and shrimp in a small amount of olive oil until 75% done. Add crab meat, onion, and spices. Continue to simmer for an additional 3 minutes and then add alfredo sauce. Allow to simmer for about 5 more minutes more or until well blended. Remove from heat. Stir and pour over fettucine noodles. Garnish with parsley flakes and serve.

Serves 2

Index by Recipe Title

Index by Category

ENTREES

Mustard Lamb Shanks 138
Pan Seared Soft Shell Crab Po Boy with
    Chayote Choux Choux 36
Pasta Mediterranean 40
Pasta Sitka 42
Crispy Fried Calamari with
    Remoulade Sauce 94
Destin Triggerfish with Lump Crab &
    Caper Meuniere 110
Fried Flounder 60
Grilled Grouper with Salsa &
    Feta Cheese 117
Grouper Elizabeth 41
Grouper Salad 16
Mahi Mahi with Pecan, Butter, &
    Frangelico Sauce 60
Pistachio Encrusted Tuna with
    Tropical Fruit Beurre Blanc 82
Potato Galette with Roasted Pepper
    & Cheese 138
Rigatoni with Roasted Chicken
    & Sweet Peppers 90
Roasted Chicken with
    Garlic & Vegetables 90
Scampi Provencal 149
Seafood Alfredo 41
Seafood Fettucine 149
Sesame Crusted Yellowfin Tuna 118
Shrimp Genoa 125
Shrimp Salad 60
Snapper Amaretto 124
Snapper Destin 52
Soft Shell Crawfish on Eggplant 52
Spinach Fettucine 136
Steak & Mushroom Pie 104
Thai Chicken 61

Veal Scotto 125

FISH

Bacon Wrapped Tuna a la Fud 66
Baked Fish 23
Baked Snapper Ricotta 126
Blackened Grouper with
    Creole Hollandaise 136
Pasta Sitka
Pistachio Encrusted Tuna with
    Tropical Fruit Beurre Blanc 82
Sesame Crusted Yellowfin Tuna 118
Shark Florida 23
Snapper Amaretto 124
Snapper Destin 52

GAME AND OTHER

Chaurice Sausage 34
Grilled Venison Sausage with
    Caramelized Onions 92
Mustard Lamb Shanks 138

GRAINS

Jambalaya 137
Par Cooked Arborio Rice 34
Rice Pilaf 118
Souffle Cornbread 37

MISCELLANEOUS

Breading for Fried Fish
Cajun Spice 47
Coconut Candy 27
Coconut Punch (Puerto Rican Egg Nog) 18
Egg Wash for Frying 60
Glazed Nuts 54
Hush Puppies 26

Shrimp Salad 60
Soft Shell Crawfish on Eggplant 52

SOUPS, STEWS, AND GUMBOS

Chicken Stock 45
Chilled Plum Soup 43
Chilled Zucchini Soup 85
Corn & Crab Chowder 55
Cream of Chicken a la Reine Soup 120
Gumbo
    Elephant Walk 42
    Captain Dave's 30
    Sunset Bay 139
Gumbo Blanc 30
Irish Stew 105
Kiss Yo' Mama Soup 37
Lentil Soup with Apple Smoked Bacon 111
Lobster Bisque 43
Oyster Stew 16
Roasted Sweet Pepper Soup 96
Seafood Bisque 97
Seafood Gumbo 139
Senate Bean Soup 105
Spicy Tomato Soup 120
Squashed Crab Soup 68
Vegetable Stock 96

VEGETABLES

Caramelized Onions 92
Couch Potatoes 69
French Bean & Corn Casserole 17
Potato Galette with Roasted Peppers
   & Cheese 138
Stuffed Roasted Peppers 110
Vegetable Stock 96

Please send_____additional copies of

The Spirit of the Place: Emerald Coast Cookbook.

Name:_____

Address_____

City_____

State_____Zip_____

18.95 per copy
1.00 (shipping)

*Florida residents add
7% sales tax (1.33 per book).*

TOTAL:_____

Send check or money order to:

Oracle Publishing Company
P.O. Box 1741
Santa Rosa Beach, FL 32459

My favorite Emerald Coast restaurants (including those in Pensacola and Panama City) are:

Please send_____additional copies of

The Spirit of the Place: Emerald Coast Cookbook.

Name:_____

Address_____

City_____

State_____Zip_____

18.95 per copy
1.00 (shipping)

*Florida residents add
7% sales tax (1.33 per book).*

TOTAL:_____

Send check or money order to:

Oracle Publishing Company
P.O. Box 1741
Santa Rosa Beach, FL 32459

My favorite Emerald Coast restaurants (including those in Pensacola and Panama City) are:

The Spirit of the Place series of cookbooks celebrates some of America's most culturally and geographically unique regions. Watch for future *Spirit of the Place* cookbook titles, each one featuring new and outstanding recipes from the celebrated restaurants of each region.

Volume I	*Florida's Emerald Coast*
Volume II	*The Florida Keys*
Volume III	*Florida's Gold Coast*
	(Miami and surrounding area)

The Spirit of the Place series of cookbooks celebrates some of America's most culturally and geographically unique regions. Watch for future *Spirit of the Place* cookbook titles, each one featuring new and outstanding recipes from the celebrated restaurants of each region.

Volume I	*Florida's Emerald Coast*
Volume II	*The Florida Keys*
Volume III	*Florida's Gold Coast*
	(Miami and surrounding area)